CREATING DEMAND

*Move the Masses to Buy
Your Product, Service, or Idea.*

RICK OTT

Ocean View Communications
A division of Symmetric Systems, Inc.
Richmond, Virginia
(800) 337-8587

Written by: Rick Ott
Original manuscript edited by: Martin Snead
Revised manuscript edited by: Rick Ott
Cover art: Brenda Shelton Martin
Cover photo: Robert Ziegler

Printed in the United States of America.

ISBN: 0-9663491-1-3

Contents

PART 5: SUSTAINING DEMAND

PART 6: GETTING HELP

Preface

Most people think of demand as an uncontrollable, obstinate force that comes and goes as it pleases. Like the Dow Jones Industrial Average (which is really only the aggregated buy/sell preferences of millions of individuals), demand is often thought of as a powerful living organism with a mind of its own. "What did the Dow do today?" one might ask. Similarly, people are always asking questions like "Is demand increasing or decreasing?" or "Is there demand for this product?" or "What is demand likely to be for kloptigobinators over the next decade?" Demand is viewed as a "given" in the equation, affecting all the other variables — including the lives of products, companies, and individuals.

Here are two better questions you can ask right now. "Is demand really such an independent, uncontrollable force, or can the marketer* exercise some control over it?" and "If it can be controlled, what can I do to create, grow, and sustain demand for my product** in a major way?"

---

*The term *marketer* refers to anyone formally or informally involved in the production and mass selling of a product, service, or oneself. Whether you're the CEO, a marketing manager or sales manager, a small business owner, a self-employed professional, a politician, actor, or anyone else interested in influencing the masses, you're a marketer.
**The terms, *product, service,* and *company* are used interchangeably.

You'll have the answer to the first question before finishing this Preface. The answer to the second question encompasses the remainder of the book.

WHAT CREATING DEMAND *ISN'T*

When I told a friend the name of this book was going to be *Creating Demand*, he said "hmm . . . sounds manipulative." If its sounds that way to you, let's set the record straight right now.

In a capitalist society, the consumer* is king. Everything is done for the benefit of consumers. Consumers determine what will be supplied by how they choose to spend their money. And make no mistake about it, consumers choose to spend their money as they please. They have options and alternatives. They choose what to buy and when to buy. They are the ultimate authority. They are in charge.

One of the underlying assumptions you must accept to be a successful marketer is that the public cannot be "manipulated." No matter how clever you are and how much money you spend you cannot exercise any "mind control" over the public and "make them buy" your product or service.

Yes, the world is full of crooks and con artists who are seemingly able to fleece the public with one crazy scam after the next. Even some straight-up marketers with legitimate products sometimes stray into the gray area of deception at times. But such practices usually don't work en masse (you can only fool some of the people), and most have flash-in-the-pan longevity (you can't fool 'em for very long).

Marketers that rely on manipulation always end up with poor sales, bad publicity, angry customers, or all three. Some end up out of business or in jail. None of which describes you, the honest-to-goodness marketer with a beneficial product or service, who wants success over the long run.

---

*The terms *consumer, customer, client,* and *buyer,* are used interchangeably.

WHAT CREATING DEMAND *IS*

Simply put, to create demand you (*a*) implement specific strategies and techniques that are designed to induce strong want and desire in a person's mind, and (*b*) execute additional techniques that cause demand to spread to many people. You, the marketer, are proactively affecting demand rather than merely reacting to whatever level of demand might otherwise exist.

Here's another way of looking at it. With the strategies and techniques presented in this book, the marketer creates demand the same way a comedian creates laughter. Both laughter and demand are inherent desires of every human being (people want to laugh and they want to consume). When a comedian is funny, he or she induces laughter in the audience. Since people like to laugh, they like the comedian and they like what he does to them. When a marketer applies the right psychological techniques, she induces desire for a particular product or service in her audience. Since people like to consume, they like what the marketer does to them, and they react by purchasing the product in question.

HOW THIS BOOK WILL HELP YOU

There's so much information on marketing floating around, it's often difficult for even the most seasoned marketers to get a handle on it. Many marketers are downright misguided and confused. They feel snowed under by the mountain of material, most of which is confusing and contradictory to begin with. As a consequence, a marketer may not know even where to begin and what steps to take.

I saw the need for one definitive source that boils it all down, that edits out all the irrelevant knowledge and presents only the essence. A book that simplifies, not complicates. A book that includes procedural steps so you know how to implement what we discuss. (Demand creation actually involves some pretty complicated psychological principles. When you're creating demand, you're operating at the high end of marketing sophistication, far beyond the old approaches of just recognizing demand and serving it. However, you need not concern yourself with the inherent complex nature the underlying principles. I've simplified it all, and present it to you in a straightforward, easy-to-grasp fashion.)

A Combination of New Innovation and Classic Wisdom

Some of the material in this book is brand-new, cutting-edge. Some of the material is classic — the accumulated wisdom of the ages. In fact, I begin with some important basics so you'll have a solid foundation in place before you get into the more advanced stuff. But all of it is extremely powerful and essential for any marketer aspiring to the highest levels of success in the 21st century.

Universal Application

Most of the material in this book has universal application, regardless of business type or size. The strategies and techniques will work for you, whether you're a one-person entrepreneur just getting started, or a top-level executive with a major corporation, or anywhere in between.

It will be up to you, however, to mold and adapt the material to your particular situation. Although I don't know what industry you're in, or what your product or service might be, I do know this: You have the ability to create, innovate, and implement effectively. You may need someone to set up the parameters and guide you along, but that's what I'm here for. By combining our mutual expertise, you will create demand like never before.

IT'S TIME TO PUSH THE GO BUTTON

Get your pen and pad of paper ready (ideas will come to you at any time; be sure to write them down or they'll get away). Fire-up the engines and hang on to your seat . . . we're about to make this demand jet soar!

Rick Ott

PART 1

SETTING YOURSELF UP FOR SUCCESS

Before you delve into the sophisticated range of high-powered demand creation, you must have a solid foundation of basics in place. Otherwise, all the sophisticated stuff won't work. Amazingly, marketers often have no problem executing the sophisticated techniques, even as they simultaneously drop the ball when it comes to the basics, thereby rendering their entire marketing effort ineffectual.

As a professional speaker, seminar leader, and consultant, I deal on a daily basis with all kinds of businesses that are seeking help in one form or another. Guess what? In three quarters of the cases, it's the basics they require. Only 25 percent of all marketers are ever ready to deal with anything beyond the basics. And those that are ready wisely "check off" on the basics first.

Chapters 1 through 4 are about setting yourself up to succeed going in. They will provide you with a solid foundation on which to build your marketing program and create the massive demand you desire.

Chapter One

The Prerequisites of Demand Creation

R ecently, I met with some very nervous owners of a CHR-formatted* radio station in a medium-sized city. The station had enjoyed high-flying success for many years, but lately they were getting killed in the ratings by a new CHR competitor. They felt the time had come to take some new and decisive measures to regain leadership. They retained my firm to help. (Although I work with companies in a variety of industries, many of my clients are radio and television stations. In broadcasting, the object is to increase ratings; to get as many people tuning in as possible. The use of consultants is very widespread in broadcasting. Just about every radio and television station has at lease one of us on the payroll.)

The meeting was a real experience. Within 15 seconds of walking into their building, I was briskly escorted down the hallway, past peeking eyeballs behind cracked doors, into a hushed "war room," where five of their top executives anxiously awaited. After a round of introductions on their part and a quick travel synopsis on my

---

*CHR stands for "Contemporary Hit Radio," called "Top 40" in the old days.

part (clients find great assurance in knowing the consultant has traveled long and far to get to their city), they began to pick up their chairs. The president of the radio division suggested we all huddle in the center of the room and speak in whispers, presumably (I gathered) to foil any cup-holding eavesdroppers behind the door or in the ventilator shaft.

For the next hour, they proceeded to tell me everything one would ever want to know about their main competitor. Speaking in military terms, they not only gave me the blow-by-blow of how the competitor "blindsided us" with a "flank attack," but they recounted every promotional stunt the competitor had ever pulled. They were especially incensed by the recent discovery that the competitor had been stealing their trash and combing it for memos. "They kept coming on the air with the exact same promotions and contests we were planning!" one of the executives declared.

Although I did find their war stories somewhat entertaining, eventually I knew it was time for me to step in and redirect the conversation. I had to get their attention off the competitor, first of all. Second, I had to focus their attention on what really matters initially: accurately assessing their own ability (or inability as the case may be) to succeed.

YOUR FIRST PRIORITY

Specifically, I wanted to find out if they had the three *prerequisites of marketing success* in place. If they did, I knew they'd get their listeners back. If they didn't, I knew they had to first get the three prerequisites in place or nothing else they did would matter. *Without the three prerequisites of success in place, success is simply not in the cards.*

The three prerequisites of success are musts for all marketers, including you, regardless of the industry you're in or the nature of your product or service. They are your first priority in demand creation.

In addition, the prerequisites of success form your main fortress of defense. When you have all three in place, you're well insulated against competitive moves, whatever they may be. If you lack any one of the prerequisites, you're vulnerable. If you lack any two, it's only a matter of time before you fall victim to a competitor. If you lack all three, you're already dead.

As we discuss each of the prerequisites of success, evaluate your own position. If you are deficient in one or more of them, please spend your time and effort acquiring the ones you don't have or beefing up the ones you do. Once you have all three prerequisites solidly in place, you'll automatically leap to the top 20 percent of all marketers in the world . . . and that's even before you begin!

PREREQUISITE NUMBER ONE: YOU MUST ADOPT A MARKETING MINDSET

It doesn't matter whether you are the chairman of the board of a multinational corporation or the sole proprietor of your own small business. It doesn't matter whether your current job title includes the word "marketing," "advertising," "promotions," or anything even remotely close. It doesn't even matter if you have any prior marketing experience. If you want to create demand (even if you won't be handling the actual duties), *you* must first adopt a marketing mindset.

What do I mean by a marketing mindset? A marketing mindset is composed of four elements:
- **1: You must acknowledge the importance of marketing.** Marketing is, or will be, responsible for a large degree of your success. And it will become increasingly so throughout the 21st century.
- **2: You must appreciate the marketing process.** Marketing — the primary elements of which are advertising, promotion, publicity, and contesting — employs some fascinating psychological principles and exciting media usage techniques. At least it's fascinating and exciting to those who are "into it." Be one of them and you'll have lots of fun along the way.
- **3: You must respect the people who create and execute.** Although you are the one who must adopt a marketing mindset, you may not be the person who does all the marketing brainwork and legwork. You may have people in your organization that do most of that. And you will certainly have people

outside your organization helping you, including the media people you deal with and any creative/production suppliers or ad agency people. A healthy display of respect and appreciation goes a long way.

- **4:You must remind yourself of the importance of marketing, your appreciation of the process, and respect for the people — daily.** You must "think marketing" all the time (not every minute of every day, of course, but at least once a day).

You can always tell when people do not have a marketing mindset in place. They're always in scramble mode, as though they wake up one morning and realize they've got to mount some sort of ad campaign by the end of the week. Also, people without a marketing mindset tend to be in a perpetual state of frustration and disappointment. They never really understand why things aren't working.

Without a marketing mindset, you'll never get your marketing program off the ground. You'll be constantly fighting with yourself and with any colleagues who do have a marketing mindset. Or you may not give much thought to marketing at all. And you'll certainly give in to the strong and recurring temptation to cut your marketing expenses. Without a marketing mindset, you'll end up sabotaging your own success time and time again.

PREREQUISITE NUMBER TWO: YOU MUST BE COMMITTED TO DEVELOPING A QUALITY PRODUCT (AND/OR SERVICE)

The quality of your product or service must be high. Obviously. Yet as obvious as it seems, an amazingly high number of marketers seem oblivious to it.

The real problem is that each legitimate marketer believes his or her product is of high quality, whether or not that is really the case. Thinking he has that base covered, he spends little energy questioning, testing, and comparing his own quality. The radio station I spoke of earlier was putting out such a bad on-air product it deserved to lose listeners. It certainly wasn't going to attract any more listeners until the product was improved considerably. And don't forget what got domestic car manufacturers into trouble in the 1970s and early

'80s. Back then General Motors, Ford, and Chrysler hadn't even heard of the word quality. It took them many years to turn that around.

So how is your product or service quality? You need to answer that from the viewpoint of your customer or consumer, not your own viewpoint. Every so often, you should pull yourself away from the day-to-day workings of your particular job and physically go out into the marketplace. Talk to your consumers, customers, clients. Observe what they do. Evaluate your product vis-a-vis the other alternatives available to the buyer. How does your product stack up? Is the quality really as good as it could be?

Quality is not as subjective as most people believe. The public has a remarkable ability to ascertain quality, and usually rather quickly. People may debate the value of product differences — Ford has its loyal fans and so does Chevrolet — but people seldom debate quality. That's one reason some products or services sell steadily year after year and others disappear as rapidly as they appeared.

When you don't have a high-quality product or service (relative to its price category), you stand to waste a lot of money attempting to create significant demand. As we all know, the best marketing in the world won't help a poor-quality product.

In years past, under the Pillsbury ownership, Burger King kept hiring and firing ad agencies and mounting new ad campaigns with rapid succession. Each go-around produced no greater sales than the previous one. Wasn't it obvious to them that advertising was not the problem? Either none of the Burger King executives actually ate at their own restaurants, or their closeness distorted their ability to conclude that room-temperature burgers and apathetic counter clerks constituted subpar quality. As is often the case with marketers that mistakenly pay poor attention to product quality, they eventually gave up and sold the chain. Actually, the entire Pillsbury company, including Burger King, was acquired by Diageo PLC (called Grand Metropolitan at the time) in 1989. Their first priority was improving Burger King's quality, and sure enough, sales began improving shortly thereafter.

One other thing: Quality can fluctuate. Sometimes you're ahead of the competition; sometimes they jump ahead of you. Sometimes your product works without a hitch; sometimes a bug appears. Notice, however, the way this prerequisite is worded. You must be committed to developing a quality product and/or service. Your commitment to quality should not waiver. If you're truly committed to having a high-quality product, on average, you'll have it.

PREREQUISITE NUMBER THREE: YOU MUST HAVE MONEY

You must have money to spend on marketing or you won't be doing much of it. You can't afford to waste time griping, moaning, and complaining about the expenditures. Nor can you afford bringing on heart attacks or ulcers every time you sign another check. No question about it — marketing costs money. Accept it and move on. That's the bad news.

The good news is that (*a*) you can probably save a good chunk of your present expenditures by eliminating waste and inefficiencies, and (*b*) you can make the dollars you do spend pay off big. (We'll discuss it all in subsequent chapters.) Your payoff can be so big, in fact, that your return on investment is nothing short of phenomenal, well worth every dollar you put in.

Say I offered you this deal: Take a $50 bill out of your wallet or purse right now and set it down in front of you. I'm going to step up and take that bill, put it in my pocket, and keep it. Then I'm going to pull a $100 bill out of my pocket and give it to you in return. Would you do that deal?

Of course you would, provided you had a fifty in your possession to begin with. And provided it was available to invest in this deal and not preallocated to something else.

Is it unrealistic to think you could realize a 100 percent return on your marketing investment? Probably. Most successful marketers realize far *greater* than 100 percent returns. The top 100 advertisers consistently average over $60 in gross revenue for every dollar of marketing expense, year after year. That's over 6,000 percent return on investment. And that's just the average. Many do better. Of course, other factors besides marketing affect sales, but the point still holds: Marketing — including its largest component, advertising — can pay off big. This book will guide you though all the right moves to make for a big payoff, but you have to supply the money to invest.

How Much Money Do You Need?

The actual amount of marketing money you need is relative. Relative to the size of your business, the industry you're in, the level of competition, and what you're trying to accomplish, just to name a few variables. Major corporations spend billions on marketing each year, and some small businesses spend just a few thousand.

So . . . how much should you budget for marketing? I wish I could spare you ambiguity, but the real answer is that you need enough money to do the job. And whatever that amount is for you, be assured that you'll get the most bang for that buck by implementing the techniques in this book. Almost all are designed to produce the highest possible results with the least amount of expenditure. Some even cost very little to implement.

Time is an Alternative

What if you simply do not have any marketing money? Does that mean you're destined for failure? Not necessarily. There is a substitute for money, and it's called time. If you don't have the money, then you'd better have lots of time (years, most likely) to grow your revenues through word-of-mouth and referral alone (which tend to be slow moving).

This book is primarily for marketers that aren't fortunate enough to have decades in which to build demand slowly, however. Most of the techniques contained herein are designed to boost demand rather quickly. If that's what you have in mind, and you've got the three prerequisites of marketing success in place, you're ready to move ahead.

Chapter Two

The Power Tools of Marketing

The Crazed Complicator inhabits small and large companies alike. He or she believes that the marketing of their product or service is, or is supposed to be, a Byzantine and convoluted process. Every working day is dedicated to that belief. With research grinding and computer whirling, the Crazed Complicator (who often goes by the title of Director of Marketing or Advertising Manager or the like) presides over a self-perpetuated mountain of information. From that perch the Crazed Complicator directs a plethora of swirling advertising and promotional maneuvers with such vigor an O'Hare air traffic controller would appear comatose by comparison.

The prime by-product of the Crazed Complicator is disorganization and confusion, though he goes to great measures to appear just the opposite. Internally, few co-workers understand what is going on, though they may have some appreciation for the Crazed Complicator's dazzling style. Out in the marketplace, people are definitely confused. But the Crazed Complicator keeps throwing so many new ads and promotions out there that some do take effect. Despite her drawbacks, the Crazed Complicator can maintain a moderate degree of success, at least until upper management discovers how fast she's chewing up the budget. (Interestingly, I've seen a few Crazed Complicators raise their own stock by purposely creating confusion. By making it appear that marketing is an overwhelmingly complex endeavor, a Crazed Complicator can sometimes snow management into believing he is the only person capable of dealing with the "enormity" of it all.)

LET SIMPLICITY BE YOUR PHILOSOPHY

You don't want to be a Crazed Complicator. Nor do you want to be intimidated by some Crazed Complicator who tries to make you feel inferior because you choose not to welter in complexity.

There is a much better approach. Its basis is simplicity. The idea is to whittle marketing down to a few easily managed parts. Then you can become good at managing those few important parts, and forget the rest. Let's whittle.

THE NON-TEXTBOOK DEFINITION

The textbook definition of marketing goes something like "all commercial activity that gets a product or service from the producer to the consumer." My definition of marketing is much more focused: persuading the masses to buy.

The difference between marketing and selling has to do with the masses. Sales is primarily a one-on-one function, salesperson to prospect. Marketing uses the media and other vehicles to reach and persuade many people — people who may not ever have any direct contact with someone from the marketer's company.

MARKETING'S FOUR PRIMARY COMPONENTS

Let's take our definition of marketing — persuading the masses to buy — and whittle it down further. The task of persuading the masses becomes a lot easier when we deal strictly with marketing's four primary components: *advertising, promotion, publicity,* and *contesting.*

These four components of marketing are the tools you will use to market your product or service.

As we discuss each tool below, note the relative emphasis placed on each. For example, you should devote roughly 50 to 60 percent of your marketing resources to advertising. You may be surprised by the emphasis some of the tools command.

TOOL NUMBER ONE: ADVERTISING

Let's define *advertising* as the purchase of exposure in media outlets. (This includes the production of ads and commercials as well as the media space and time.) A media outlet is an individual magazine, newspaper, radio station, television network, or the like. (Print is a medium; newspapers are media; *The Washington Post* is a media outlet.)

About 50 to 60 percent of your marketing resources should be allocated to advertising. It is your number one tool in demand creation. That's because advertising has two big advantages:

- **Advertising is controlled by the marketer.** You control not only the message, but also the level of exposure.

- **Advertising has the potential to reach and affect mass numbers of people quickly.** When done correctly, advertising can produce tremendous results in a relatively short period of time.

Advertising's biggest drawback is that it costs money — sometimes big money — to reach the level at which results kick in and the ad expenditures pay off. As I mentioned earlier, there are two primary ways of making your expenditures pay off big: cutting wasted spending and improving each ad's effectiveness. Chapter 4 is devoted entirely to cutting waste. Throughout other chapters, you'll find numerous techniques, some with incredible power, to boost the effectiveness of your advertising.

TOOL NUMBER TWO: PROMOTIONS

A *promotion* (noun) is an event requiring attendance and/or other kinds of participation on the part of the public (or your target consumer). A contest is a promotion, as a truck is a vehicle. But not all promotions are contests, as not all vehicles are trucks. Contests warrant their own category, so well discuss them later.

Promotions should garner about 20 to 30 percent of your marketing resources.

There are three types of promotional events: *self-sponsored, co-sponsored,* and *ride-along.* Each differs based on the role, or degree of sponsorship, the marketer assumes.

Self-sponsored promotions are events you create, organize, execute, and finance yourself. Say, for example, a gift shop has an open house one weekend. Or a radio station puts on a raft race. Or a soft drink stages "taste tests" around the country. Or a cable network sponsors a jazz festival. These are all examples of promotions in which the marketer assumes the role of sole or primary sponsor. (The sponsor may, of course, sell secondary sponsorships to other marketers if it so chooses.)

Co-sponsored promotions, sometimes called partnership promotions, are events in which two or more marketers join together and assume equal sponsorship roles. Each marketer brings its expertise and money to the table, and each shares in the benefits. For instance, McDonald's and Disney often work together on movie promotions. Or a radio station and a night club throw a party. Or a newspaper and a shopping mall co-sponsor a technology fair. If you've noticed in these examples, the optimum combination of co-promoters is when one is a media outlet and the other has high-traffic locations.

Ride-along promotions are events sponsored by another party, but in which the marketer participates. In many cases, the participating marketer pays a fee to the sponsor in exchange for involvement. There's no better example of this than the Super Bowl, where various marketers pay the NFL (the owner of the event) for the right to be involved.

TOOL NUMBER THREE: PUBLICITY

Publicity is defined as non-purchased exposure in the news, editorial, or noncommercial section of a media outlet's material.

Publicity should get about 5 to 10 percent of your marketing resources. Since publicity, by definition, is non-purchased exposure, your dollar expenditures on it will go to creating and disseminating information about your product, service, or business, rather than buying space or time.

Publicity Can be Dangerous

Marketers can become seduced by the allure of favorable publicity. In fact, they can become obsessed with it. Like the compulsive gambler who's driven by the hope of hitting the jackpot, a publicity-driven marketer can end up spending way too much time and money trying to generate it . . . and can end up losing badly in many ways.

Perhaps the "gobs of wonderful publicity" you were hoping for will turn out to be but a token mention in some generic fashion. For example, the newspaper article might report the big, citywide clothing drive by noting "a thousand dollars worth of brand new casual wear was donated by a local clothing merchant" (that's you).

Or a feature story about you in a local magazine finally comes out, and lo and behold, you can't believe your eyes! How could that nice reporter who spent two days as your best buddy write such a scathing exposé? Not only does the story rip you to shreds, but they used an unflattering photo of you in a goofy pose that was taken as part of the "test shots" before the "real shots" were supposedly taken.

Or one of those syndicated television tabloid shows get ahold of a document you should have shredded, a tape you should have erased, or an ex-employee you shouldn't have crossed, and in one day's time you go from a low-profile, out-of-court settler to a high-profile, nationally-known bonehead.

Or, you got lucky and received a good amount of coverage in a positive vein. This happens about 20 percent of the time.

You Have No Control

Unlike advertising, which the marketer controls, publicity is totally out of the marketer's control. The newspaper, magazine, radio, or television station granting the publicity is in total control. Reporters and writers can say almost anything they please about you or your company. If you're a "public figure," they can even go so far as to make up things about you, or use you as the butt of jokes.

When a marketer becomes a "victim of negative press," she often reels into shock or befuddlement. "How could this happen?" she wonders incredulously. She may get angry and attempt to retaliate. Cancelling one's advertising on the offending media outlet is a common response, though some people take it further with threatened or actual lawsuits.

I experienced an interesting incident in the early '70s when I was a disc jockey in Lansing, Michigan. The guy who did the news during my airshift led his 3:30 P.M. newscast with a story on a local car dealer that got caught turning back the odometer on used cars. Not the biggest news event ever to hit Lansing, but it must have been a slow news day. Anyway, the newsman delivered the story like it was the biggest news story of the year, complete with phrases like "caught red-handed" and "ripping off the public."

Well, guess who was the sponsor of the newscast? That's right, it was indeed the car dealer. As the newsman finished the odometer story, he paused and said "more news after this," a standard line going into a commercial. I fired off the tape, and there's the car dealer himself talking about his wonderful selection of low-milage used cars.

The next thing I know Mr. Low Milage is on the hitline screaming louder and faster than he did in his commercials (and using a few expletives I did not recall as part of his commercial vocabulary). I told him this was the request line and I'd be happy to get a song on for him; otherwise he'd have to call the business office — which he must have done, since we never ran his commercials after that. (He eventually returned to the air when the station salesperson convinced him he needed even more commercials now to counteract the ill effects of the hatchet job.)

Why is There So Much Negative Publicity?

Turn on the television, read today's newspaper, pick up any magazine . . . and notice how often people, products, or companies are portrayed in negative light. Why is negativity so prevalent? Let me answer by first pointing out my position. I speak as a marketer myself, a consultant to other marketers, and as a professional speaker and writer. I have an extensive media background, which includes broadcast journalism. I'll take no sides in this discussion, but present it from all sides.

The four main reasons why negative publicity exists:

- **A media outlet may be uninformed or misinformed.** A writer or reporter needs information, but it won't necessarily be all the information you'd like them to have. Do not assume any media people know about you or all the good things you're up to. It's not incumbent upon the media to seek out favorable information about you; it's incumbent upon you to provide them with favorable information.
- **The marketer and the media have different, and often opposing, goals.** The marketer is focused on getting favorable media exposure, but the media couldn't care less about that. The media want to disseminate information that (*a*) tells people something they don't already know, and (*b*) affects as many people as possible.

  The media hate pointing out the obvious. They yearn to point out, or "uncover," the opposite of the obvious. So if the general consensus about you is favorable, what good does it do any media outlet to further that line of thinking?

  Look at the way the media cover the president of the United States (whoever may occupy that position at any point in time). The president is always trying to show himself in the best light possible, and the media is always searching for information to the contrary. When they find something, however trivial it may be, they milk it for all it's worth, sometimes turning a tidbit into a mountain. Why? You know the answer: the media want to tell people something new, and new information is almost always the opposite of the prevailing information.

For many years, Donald Trump demonstrated a masterful ability to generate favorable publicity. With every new and bigger project he undertook, his publicity grew proportionally. But as Trump became so well-known as the squeaky clean, megarich hotel/casino magnate extraordinare, the media became increasingly hungry for information to the contrary. Like a boulder that is pushed up a mountain side by the marketer, publicity will eventually turn in direction and come roaring down with a velocity equal to its height, often crushing the marketer in its wake. Lo and behold, in 1990, when Trump ran into difficulty with his marriage and his finances, the salivating media pounced. Trump and all his problems became the biggest news story of the year, it seemed. Only when Iraq invaded Kuwait, and the Gulf War began in 1991, did a story come along that eclipsed that of Donald Trump.

Mike Wallace of CBS's "60 Minutes" explained the relationship between the marketer and the media this way: "What they want is to promote their book or show or political view, and there's an exchange. What we want is to get beneath the facade."

So the next time you reach out to the media in hopes of generating favorable publicity, keep this in mind: While you're trying to present your best, the media is trying to get beneath it all.

- **People see things differently.** Why is it that two different witnesses to the same automobile accident tell completely different renditions of what happened? For whatever reasons, people see things differently. That's why two or more reporters can cover the same story and write vastly different accounts. That's why a reporter or writer might do a story on you (or your product, service, or business) that turns out to be quite opposite of how you or the next guy would write about you.

But what about the facts, you ask? How could a writer or reporter distort the facts so blatantly? You'd better sit down for this: The actual "facts" do not exist. The "facts" are, in reality, whatever a person believes them to be. There are no more vivid examples of this phenomenon than can be witnessed every day in the legal profession. The prosecution and the defence present completely different sets of "facts," that each seem believable. One side believes in its "facts," and the other it its "facts." As it turns out, fact is based on belief, not the other way around.

- **A media outlet's angle may be opposite the marketer's angle.** Many ideas for feature stories or articles come from the media people themselves, not from news events per se. So instead of waiting for something to happen and simply covering it, a reported may decide to proactively prepare a feature on "the corruption in city hall," for example, and then proceed to dig up information that supports that story line.

Let's say a newspaper reporter calls and wants to interview you. "Great!" you reason. "We could certainly use the publicity." You show the reporter around your restaurant and spend another hour answering questions in your office while a photographer is snapping away all along. The article comes out a couple weeks later, and all that great publicity you (naively) expected is nothing of the sort. The angle of the article is the health hazards of high-cholesterol restaurant food, and there's a photo of your cook pouring cheese over eggs with a caption that reads "Patrons of restaurants like Joe's Eatery have no idea how much fat goes into their food."

Is it fair? Is it right? It's certainly debatable. Remember, the reporter's loyalty is to her employer, and the employer's (the media outlet's) loyalty is to its audience. They have no loyalty or obligation to the person they're interviewing.

The next time you read an unfavorable article about a company in *Forbes*, or watch a revealing exposé on "Dateline," ask yourself this: did the reporter call up and say "I'd like to interview you for a negative article I'm writing that will surely make you look like a total buffoon"? Hardly. The reporter never let on that the story would take a negative slant (the reporter may not even have known it would end up being negative going in). Although the marketer might object to such reporting tactics, the public — whom the media outlets serve — might be very appreciative.

How to Generate Favorable Publicity

Publicity is very iffy — you can't rely on it to be there when you need it, and you can't rely on it to be positive. That's why it warrants only a small percent of your marketing resources. However, there are some things you can do to generate favorable publicity so that the small amount of it you do get works in your favor.

- **Don't do anything that warrants negative publicity.** If you've been turning back odometers, you have no right to complain when the media get hold of it. If you're having improper relations with an intern, and you happen to be president of the United States, know that the media will expose you sooner or later (and when they do, you're likely to be in serious trouble). The higher your profile, the cleaner you need be.
- **Be honest with the media.** Of course, you needn't volunteer negative information or tell tales out of school. It's okay to put your best foot forward, or to even be a bit evasive or coy. Just don't tell blatant lies. A lie will always come back to haunt you, and usually with great magnitude. Remember, hell hath no fury like a reporter duped.
- **Keep the press informed.** Sure, ninety-five percent of all "news releases" that reach an editor's desk go straight into the waste basket. But they are read first. And some — the five percent — get acted upon. Send information to key reporters or editors from time to time, even though most of it generates nothing. You never know when an interest will be sparked and a story will result.
- **Become a quotable "source."** Reporters quote knowledgeable people all the time (many media outlets require reporters or writers to quote *x* number of "experts or "authorities" in each piece as a measure of good reporting). Part of the material you send to the media should contain quotes from you that may be lifted and used as the writer sees fit. In time, they may call you and ask for your comments regarding some news event. One media outlet sees you quoted in another, and soon you're a legitimate "source" on numerous contact databases. (All of this presumes you have something intelligent and worthwhile to say.)

- **Submit material for publication.** Instead of waiting for them to do a story on you, you do a story on you. Write an article and submit it along with a photo. Many publications have regular columns set up to feature guest authors. Television stations use footage supplied by marketers all the time (saves them the trouble of generating it themselves).

- **Avoid stunting.** Publicity stunts are very risky in that the media view them as cheap attempts to get attention for no other reason than the exposure. You can end up looking very foolish very quickly. (And that's if the media decides to give you some exposure. Most of the time, they ignore publicity stunts altogether.)

  There is an exception. If you're in the entertainment industry, or you thrive on flamboyance for whatever reason, you can successfully mount some "wild and crazy" stunt from time to time. For example, radio personalities are always doing some stunting, such as camping out on a billboard for a week, burying oneself underground for a few days, or riding a rollercoaster for eight hours straight. Most often, though, such stunts are done in the name of fund raising for some charitable cause. It's difficult for a media outlet to ignore or criticize a publicity seeker when the seeker is acting on behalf of a charity.

And when you do get hit by some negative publicity . . .

- **Let negative publicity roll off your back.** If you're a player, you're going to be tackled for a loss from time to time. Sooner or later, you'll be hit by a negative story, if for no other reason than you're visible and therefore a target. When it happens, you've got to maintain your cool and go about your business as usual. Avoid retaliating, although an unemotional letter correcting any erroneous information may be appropriate. The same media outlet that burns you one day can embrace you the next. Reporters and writers come and go, and yesterday's news is ancient history. Don't prevent yourself from getting positive press in the future by going into a tyrannical rage every time a negative comment is made about you.

TOOL NUMBER FOUR: CONTESTS

Contests? A marketing power tool? Absolutely. And yes, contesting is greatly undervalued by many marketers. I'm sure you've heard the arguments against contesting. They run something like this:

> "The public is tired of them."
>
> "Very few people actually participate."
>
> "A contest cheapens the image of our product."
>
> "There's no way a small firm like ours can match the magnitude of prizes offered by the big guys."
>
> "They require too much effort for too little benefit."
>
> "Why should I give away my product? I could go broke doing that."

Actually, all of these assessments can turn out to be accurate if a contest is poorly conceived or poorly executed. But for well-designed, well-executed contests, the advantages are numerous.

The day people no longer appreciate entering and winning a contest, or when they no longer enjoy having a little fun in the process, will be the day you can stop doing contests. You'll know when that day occurs, as people will suddenly stop watching "Wheel of Fortune" and "Jeopardy," stop buying state lottery tickets, and stop visiting casinos across the country.

The truth is, people never tire of the chance to win something. Because we live in a society that trades value for value, we learn "there's no such thing as a free lunch" and "nothing in the world comes free" very early in life. Anytime a person actually does get something for nothing, as occurs when they win a contest, it's always a pleasurable and memorable experience.

That's exactly why the magnitude of your prizes is virtually irrelevant. Let's say you walk into a grocery store and a sounder of some kind goes off. The manager comes up to you and says "Congratulations! You're our one hundred thousandth customer! You've just won a certificate for $100 in free groceries!" Are you likely to shove the certificate back in his face, declaring in disgust, "How dare you give me only $100 worth of free groceries! I want $17 million like the state lottery is offering!"? Or would you be excited about your good fortune, appreciate the $100 in free groceries, and tell all your friends, neighbors, and coworkers about this unexpected piece of good fortune?

It is true that very few people, relative to the entire population, participate in contests. But very few people, relative to the entire population, do anything. The purpose of a contest is not to involve the masses, anyway. It's to create excitement, add spunk and vitality to your marketing, foster positive word-of-mouth, and to collect names and addresses for your internal database (more on this later).

Three Types of Contests

Contests can take any one of three forms: *revolving, perennial,* and *one-shot.* The main difference is how often they're conducted.

Revolving contests are ongoing for an extended length of time (they may not have any predetermined end). A home improvement center, for example, may run a "Weekly Fixit" contest and give away $75 worth of merchandise each week to a customer whose name is drawn from a barrel (the more times you enter the store, the more times you can enter). A radio or television station may run a "Free Lunch" contest in which one business or office is awarded lunch for six at a local restaurant (this is also an example of a co-sponsored promotion). An apartment complex may award one month's free rent to a different tenant each month.

A perennial contest occurs each year at the same time. It's a promotional tradition. Most often perennials are built around holidays, although that is not mandatory. Miller Lite runs a Super Bowl contest every year. Many small businesses run Fourth of July, Halloween, or Christmas contests every year. Perennial contests usually build in participation with each year's successive running, making them all the more valuable over time.

One-shot contests come and go, lasting only a few weeks in duration. They are not scheduled to last or repeat, although a marketer may elect to bring back a successful one-shot contest some time in the future.

How to Run a Contest

Keep these points in mind regarding contests:
- **Use a combination of contest types.** Have one revolving contest in effect most of the time. Create some good promotional traditions with two or three perennials. Then leave yourself open for one or two one-shots a year. (You may not plan any specific one-shots in advance, but wait to take advantage of them as opportunities and ideas present themselves.)
- **Use a simple participation structure.** If you have trouble getting people to participate, it's probably because your contest takes too much effort to enter. Anything more than simply filling out an entry blank or guessing a simple answer to too complex.
- **Make your procedures incredibly clear.** How many contests have you not entered only because you weren't clear on what it is you're supposed to do to enter and win? If a person can't grasp the essence of your contest in the first four seconds, and understand how to enter and win within the first 15 seconds, it's not explained clearly enough.
- **Have lots of winners.** Many smaller-prize winners are always better than fewer larger-prize winners. If you've ever played the slot machines at a casino, you know they pay off in small increments all the time. And once in a while they pay off big. The possibility of winning the big jackpot may attract you to begin with, but the small payoffs along the way keep you interested and playing for longer lengths of time.

Multiple Payoffs For You!

Contests are a great way of attracting new customers and getting existing customers to increase their patronage. In addition, contest entry blanks are a primary vehicle for collecting names for your in-house database. Each of these benefits will be discussed further in subsequent chapters.

Chapter Three

Preparing Your Product or Service for Lift-Off

You are a model rocket hobbyist. You've entered the latest competition sponsored by your club. Your goal is to build a rocket and launch it to go as high as possible, higher than any other contestant, thereby winning the contest.

You and the other contestants will be setting up your rockets in the same general area, a grassy flat of land free of obstruction. As you look around, you notice a hill about 100 feet away. The hill is a good 20 feet higher in elevation than the area in which everyone is setting up, and a thought goes through your mind. "How much higher would my rocket go," you wonder, "if I launched from the top of the hill instead of the flatland?"

Whatever height it might reach, it would be 20 feet higher if launched from the hilltop, all others factors being equal. The problem with this idea however, is obvious. The rules of the contest prohibit one contestant from having an unfair advantage over the others, so the hilltop is off limits. You're left to rely on sheer thrust, as little wind resistance as possible, and plain old good luck to win.

But when it comes to launching the marketing rocket for your product or service, there are no rules prohibiting you — or anyone else — from launching from as high a hilltop as you can find. No one says you have to rely strictly on the power of your engine or good luck. You can put yourself at great advantage by first climbing the hill, then launching. That way, *the same amount of marketing thrust produces a much greater result.*

YOUR PRODUCT OR SERVICE MUST BE DIFFERENT

Properly preparing your product or service before you begin marketing is the equivalent of climbing to the hilltop. And the single most important way to prepare your product or service is to create differences between your product or service and others available in the marketplace. The greater the differences, the higher the hill on which you stand and the greater results you'll achieve.

Marketers often make the mistake of relying too heavily on their marketing to create the perception of differences, where no real differences exist. This is like launching your rocket from the bottom of a canyon. You need a whole lot of engine thrust just to get out of the hole, let alone high above the ground. Even the most powerful marketing engines fail when the task is just too great. Don't place unfair burden on your marketing program. Create real differences, such as those I describe below, and you'll be well ahead of the game.

THREE TYPES OF DIFFERENCES

There are three types of differences you can create: *product and/or service, container,* and *distribution.*

Product/Service Differences

Product and/or service differences are, not surprisingly, those that are inherent in your actual product or service.

In 1985, Miller Brewing Company introduced a new brand of beer called Miller Genuine Draft. To make it different from any other kind of beer, they created a process called "cold filtering."

Pert shampoo sold poorly until Proctor & Gamble created a major product difference. They made it a shampoo and conditioner in one, renaming it Pert Plus. It became the nation's best-selling shampoo.

Motown Records was founded upon the creation of a different type of music, the "street sound" of Detroit. A&M Records' first product was the unusual sound of Herb Alpert & The Tijuana Brass. Casablanca pioneered disco. Island Records pioneered reggae; Delicious Vinyl, rap. If you want to launch a new record label with the best chances of success, the more different your acts sound, the better.

Each brand of cigarette must have a product difference, or it won't sell. So some are longer, shorter, or thinner; use less tar and nicotine; sell more to a pack; or have a bigger filter, no filter, menthol taste, and so on. I'm waiting for someone to launch a square cigarette. Not that square has any practical advantage over round (won't roll off the table, perhaps?), but it would be a major difference. Remember, product and/or service differences are just that — differences. The differences needn't necessarily be improvements or advantages, though it's much better if they are. Ivory soap floats. A neat difference, but does that make Ivory a better soap? Who knows?

It's not difficult to create service differences. In fact, the simpler the idea, the better. Ukrops supermarkets (exclusive to Richmond, Virginia and the surrounding area) has people that take your groceries out to your car for you. No tipping allowed; it's just part of the extra service you get a Ukrops. I know a guy that sells automobile sound equipment, and to differentiate himself from much larger competitors, he created a major service difference. He comes to your home or workplace and installs the stuff right there, saving you the trouble of taking your car in to have the installation done.

Container Differences

Container differences are those that affect the physical package or appearance of your product.

Some recording artists try to look as different as possible. Elvis Presley looked different when he first appeared. So did Little Richard, The Beatles, David Bowie, Alice Cooper, Madonna, Boy George, and a host of others. Their different, and oftentimes outrageous, appearance means they don't have to rely strictly on their music to command attention.

Pringles potato chips come evenly stacked in a can. Pearl Drops tooth polish is a liquid that comes in a squeeze bottle (these are also examples of product differences). Duracell has a battery tester built right into its container.

Apple's iMac computer — with the translucent cover and round mouse — looks quite different. You can buy Windex in a special plastic bottle that attaches to your garden hose and squirts directly onto your outside windows. Domino's delivers your pizza in a unique "heat wave" container that keeps it extra hot.

People are better able to remember your product, and may indeed be attracted to it, based largely on your container difference(s).

Distribution Differences

Distribution differences are those that deal with how your product or service reaches the consumer, or how it is purchased.

Domino's Pizza pioneered the concept of home delivered pizza, a major difference between Domino's and others. Yet for years many people told Domino's founder Tom Monaghan he should set up tables in his stores to capture some of the dine-in crowd as well as the eat-at-home people. Domino's could, after all, continue to deliver to those that phone ordered, so the additional dine-in business would be that much better, right? Perhaps, but Tom knew that if he did that, he'd suddenly appear to be just like every other pizza restaurant. The delivery feature would get lost; it would no longer be a powerful differentiator. Quite often, a major difference is defined by what you *don't do* as well as what you do do.

John Paul Mitchell knew he'd never get anywhere selling his line of hair care products in department, drug, and grocery stores. Competing against the likes of Proctor & Gamble, Alberto-Culver, Unilever, Gillette, and other gigantic companies for shelf space alone would be next to impossible. So he decided to sell strictly to hair salons. The salons, after all, are dealing with the end user every day, and therefore in excellent position to retail the product. In addition, the salons are motivated to do so because they want another profit center besides haircuts.

Years ago, marketers such as Avon, Amway, and Tupperware decided the best way to compete in their respective industries was to use a different channel of distribution. So they each avoided the department and discount stores and chose door-to-door sales. Snap-On Tools sells and distributes from their own fleet of trucks, going straight to the buyer's (professional mechanics) place of business.

The Home Shopping Club and QVC took television advertising to its extreme by creating their own cable channels and producing 24-hour-a-day, 7-day-a-week perpetual motion commercials. Not only did they avoid the department and discount store channel, they avoided door-to-door selling.

More and more businesses are selling from their web sites. Dell Computer sells a ton of computers from its site, with their added build-to-order service that customizes the computer(s) for each buyer. And maybe you purchased this very book from one of the online booksellers, or from RickOtt.com. I actually use many different distribution channels for my books and tapes, including retail book stores, mail order catalogs, direct-response marketing, and the internet.

MULTIPLE DIFFERENCES

Can you create all three — product/service, container, and distribution differences — for one product or service? Absolutely. Having one difference in each category gives you the ultimate advantage.

The classic case, used in just about every marketing class from 1974 on, is that of L'eggs pantyhose. Prior to the introduction of L'eggs in 1970, the women's hosiery market was mature and stagnant. When the market isn't growing, you're forced to create major differences if you're to have any hope of survival, let alone major success. L'eggs did such a good job creating differences that it became the best-selling hosiery brand in the country in less than one year after introduction. Let's look at how it created various differences.

L'eggs decided from the start to create a radical product difference. Every other brand of hose was made with a non-stretch material, and came flat, in the shape of a leg. So L'eggs did the opposite. It used a stretchy material, and the product came crumpled up in a ball. They played up the product's stretchiness, using the slogan "Our L'eggs fit your legs."

Their container difference was a natural extension of the product's unique look. Whereas other brands came in flat, two-dimensional cardboard packages, L'eggs came in three-dimensional plastic eggs — not only totally different, but highly recognizable in stores. (Cardboard eggs have replaced the plastic ones in recent years. At least they're still three-dimensional and not flat.)

Then L'eggs added a major distribution difference. Every other brand of hosiery was sold in department and specialty stores. So L'eggs did the opposite. It set up point-of-purchase displays called "L'eggs Boutiques" in grocery and drug stores, circumventing the department and specialty stores completely. Keep in mind, this was a radical departure form the norm back then. L'eggs even took it one step further and set up its own fleet of trucks that pulled up *in front* of each store and delivered through the front door instead of the back door, for increased visibility. (They even went one step beyond that by using female drivers who wore the product and skin-tight hot pants — a surefire attention-getter.)

TURN MUNDANE INTO MAGIC

Some marketers might believe it's awfully difficult to create any significant difference for the less exotic, more mundane product or service. After all, a toothbrush is a toothbrush.

Yet Johnson & Johnson altered the basic toothbrush design significantly and came up with the Reach, the first brand of toothbrush to look different in about two thousand years.

I can't think of a more mundane item than a shower head. It's nothing but a pipe end with holes. Yet Teledyne saw the opportunity to create a product difference so great it ended up with a whole new product, the Shower Massage. Black & Decker updated its line of tools with the VersaPak removable battery system. Reebok added an air pump to a shoe and called it — what else — "the Pump."

Never dismiss the opportunity to create differences, no matter how mundane your product or service. In fact, a major difference can wake up a sleepy product and boost sales quickly. Also, by creating significant differences, you may be able to elevate your product or service out of the commodity category, and thereby raise its selling price.

CREATING YOUR DIFFERENCES

As you think of ways to make your product or service different in the three categories we discussed, keep these points in mind:
- **Strive for one difference per category.** Ideally, you have one product/service difference, one container difference, and one distribution difference. All three need not be monumental, though one of the three should be strong enough to dominate. More than one difference per category can become unwieldy and can dilute the total impact of the differences.
- **More is not necessarily better.** If you can't create one difference in each category, that's okay. It's better to have one major difference than to have multiple smaller differences in a variety of categories.
- **Don't fall into the "It's not done that way in my industry" trap.** If you determine that an idea is not feasible because it's not done that way in your industry, give it more consideration before dismissing it. Remember, if it's not done that way, you have a major opportunity to do it that way. Think of L'eggs, which broke all the rules and became an overnight success.
- **Don't worry about how the competition will react.** Your competitors will do one of two things: They'll either ignore your differences or they'll copy your differences. Let's look at how each affects you.
    If your competitors ignore you, the good news is that your differences will remain differences. The bad news is that you're on an independent crusade, devoid of any colleague corroboration, constantly having to "prove" that your differences really are better. Starbucks coffee, Harley-Davidson motorcycles, Claussen pickles, and Macintosh computers are uniquely-different products. Yet each must constantly sell and resell its dif-

ferences to justify its relatively higher price.

If they copy you, the good news is that they're helping "legitimize" your differences, and may thus help create a much bigger pie in which your slice and their slice both grow. The bad news is that your difference(s) will not be as great; they'll lose some effectiveness. Miller Lite was out for only a short time before other "light" beers appeared. (Miller Lite wasn't even the first light beer, just the first successful one.) FedEx had the overnight package delivery business to itself for only a short time before UPS, Airborne, the U.S. Postal Service, and others joined in. Domino's delivers, but now Pizza Hut and Papa John's does the same. L'eggs may have been the innovators extraordinaire, but it didn't take long for No Nonsense to match them step for step.

The bottom line: It doesn't matter what your competitors do. Let them do what they will. Your strategy is to do what's best for you, and that's to create good differences that give you a distinctive edge, one way or another.

Chapter Four

The Six Biggest Wastes of Marketing Money

To create massive demand, you must make sure every marketing dollar you spend, especially in the advertising and promotion areas, is working for you. No marketer ever argues with that statement. Yet many well-intended marketers end up wasting their precious financial resources on things that are simply not destined to ever produce results.

Here are the six biggest wastes of marketing money. Avoid these budget drainers, and you'll move into the top 10 percent of all marketers in the world.

WASTE NUMBER ONE: MARKETING SHORT OF THE RESULTS THRESHOLD

In football, you score points only when you get the ball over your opponent's goal line. March the ball 99 yards downfield, but fail to get it over the goal line, and you get no points. All that effort consumed by your 99-yard drive did you no good. You score the points, and receive the subsequent recognition and glory, only when you achieve that final yard and break the plane of the goal.

Marketing works the same way. You get results only when you burst through the results threshold. Stop short of the results threshold, and all the money you've spent getting 99 percent of the way there does you little good, and is therefore wasted.

The $75 Ticket to Nowhere

Let me illustrate how this happens. Say your objective is to fly from New York to London. At Kennedy Airport, you have your choice of airliners. Jet A, fueled and ready to go, costs $1,000 a ticket. Jet B, also fueled and ready to go, costs only $750 a ticket. But there's a problem with Jet B. It only has enough fuel to fly three-quarters of the way there. Of course, you'd save $250 if you took it instead of Jet A, but you would also end up sitting on a life raft in the ocean instead of in London.

Which jet would you choose, A or B? I actually asked this question in my "Creating Demand" seminar one day, and someone in the audience decided to grab the cheap laugh bait and shout "Jet B! Jet B! Hawr Hawr Hawr!" I've noticed some interesting similarities among people who go for a cheap laugh. They're almost always male; they always sit in the back of the room; and, from the evidence I've seen, they're in some sort of financial trouble. The guy who yelled "Jet B" must have indeed taken it, because his company filed for bankruptcy four months later.

Back to the action. There you are, comfortably buckled into your window seat in Jet A awaiting takeoff, wondering how Hawr-Hawr is doing over there in Jet B. The jets take off, both flying just as high and just as fast. Which one of you looks like the smarter traveler? You in your $1,000 seat or Hawr-Hawr in his $750 seat? For three-quarters of the trip, he's sitting pretty with $250 savings in his pocket. Eventually, of course, you'll arrive in London on schedule, and he'll be awaiting rescue in the ocean. You win in the end — but during the first three-quarters of the journey the illusion was that he was ahead.

For some marketers, the consequences of the $750 ticket are not obvious. They become fooled by the apparent financial "savings" at the outset and the phantom payoffs along the way. The feedback they receive from friends, family, colleagues, and even competitors gives them a false perception of major impact ("Hey, Fred, I saw your commercial on TV last night!"). Even when it becomes obvious they'll never arrive, they still find solace in the illusionary "benefits" of getting three-quarters of the way there. They buy the $750 ticket to nowhere again and again, spend a lot of time and money, yet never get much result.

Do it big

Although it may sometimes appear otherwise with marketing, especially with advertising, there are no significant incremental payoffs along the way. The payoffs are all at the end, when you finally burst through the results threshold.

To burst through the results threshold, and create the demand necessary to move the sales needle, you've got to *reach into the depths of the marketplace and impact mass numbers of people.* Even if you have a limited target market, you still have to reach the majority of people in that camp.

What does this mean as far as your marketing program goes? It means you must do it big. Make major impact. Reach critical mass. Anything else is a watered-down effort, a $750 ticket to nowhere.

The Mitigation Effect

Your marketing effort, no matter how good it is, will have a lessened impact when it goes into operation. This is a natural phenomenon called *The Mitigation Effect.* It's simply an inefficiency factor, not unlike the wires that carry electricity to your house. There's resistance in those wires, causing the electricity to lose some of its punch as it travels from the power plant to you. That's why your electric company shoots out more power than you will actually use. If they shot out only enough to match what you're supposed to get, you'd get 95 volts coming out of your wall socket instead of 110, the difference having been eaten up by the inefficiency factor.

Because of The Mitigation Effect, your marketing activity — advertising promotions, publicity, and contests — will suffer an impact reduction of some degree out in the marketplace. (This is why an ad, commercial, or billboard design always looks better in the confines of a board room than it does once it hits the streets.)

You may think you're "blowing the market wide open" when, in fact, you're really making a minimal impact. What seems like enough going in turns out not to be enough coming out. You must compensate for The Mitigation Effect by boosting your marketing activity a little above that which you think is enough.

WASTE NUMBER TWO: USING A WEAK OR CONFUSING MESSAGE

The second-biggest waste of marketing money occurs when your message is weak and/or confusing. Remember, your media buys cost the same whether you have a strong, cohesive message or a weak, confusing message. I know of no media outlet that'll say "We were going to charge you $800 a pop to run this commercial . . . but since it really stinks we'll only charge you $500."

So you pay a good amount for media exposure, yet that exposure does you little good because your message is weak. That's a waste of marketing money, and it happens all the time.

In any given day, you and I could point out a number of weak or confusing ads we happen to see or hear (we'd have to be consciously looking for them, since their weak message would more than likely render them decidedly underwhelming). A few years ago Prudential Insurance ran a campaign with a slogan that said "We won't let you get it until you've got it." What? The first time I heard it I thought perhaps I was at fault; I must have missed something. Then I heard NBC's Bob Costas recite the slogan on a football postgame show, after which he added, "frankly, I don't get it . . . but that's what it says here." Well, Bob, you and I aren't alone. No one got it. The campaign or the slogan. For a slogan to be effective, it must have self-contained clarity. Prudential's was exactly the opposite.

A billboard and radio campaign for Aunt Sarah's Pancake House confused the few people who became aware of it. The billboard version featured a big headline that read, "Don't Eat At Aunt Sarah's." A smaller line below read, "The National Junk Food Association." I asked a few people what they thought the billboard meant. One gentleman said he thought The National Junk Food Association was some watchdog agency that found Aunt Sarah's in violation of healthy food standards. He planned to do as the board suggested: avoid eating at Aunt Sarah's. A woman said she thought Aunt Sarah's must have put up the board, but was confused as to why they didn't want people to eat there. Another woman said she didn't like junk food, so she was going to avoid Aunt Sarah's. If you take the time to decipher the message, you may be able to understand what Aunt Sarah's was trying to say. But who's going to bother to do that?

Have you ever received a direct mail piece that didn't clearly indicate who the sender was, or what it was trying to sell, or what it wanted you, the recipient, to do? Just the other day I received a flyer in the mail from some marketer touting its upcoming "12 Hour Sale" with "Savings of 25 to 30 percent off our entire stock!" Although the logo was in plain sight, that didn't tell me who they were or what business they were in. I'd never heard of them before, and after reading their direct mail piece, I still don't know who they are or what they're selling.

All too often, a marketer assumes the receiver of its message (a) is paying attention, (b) cares about receiving the advertising message, (c) cares about the product or service advertised, and (d) has some prior knowledge of who the advertiser is and what the product is all about. Nothing could be further from the truth.

In reality, the percentage of people who know what you're all about and actually care is very small. To the majority of people in your target market, your ads may very well be too weak or confusing to register.

I'm not saying you shouldn't be creative or subtle. Creativity and subtlety are useful at times. But anytime creativity or subtlety gets in the way of clarity, you're reducing the effectiveness of your message by 90 percent.

Remember, very few people are going to bother to decipher what it is you're trying to get across. They've got better things to do with their time and attention. Which means you had better be clear, concise, and to the point to make an effective impression.

WASTE NUMBER THREE: MARKETING TURMOIL

The third biggest waste of marketing money occurs when you constantly change your advertising and promotional campaigns, never giving any one of them a chance to catch hold and grow. This is like constantly uprooting crops before they're ripe; you're forever sowing but never reaping.

Demand creation is a building process. Many of the techniques have cumulative effects that build and intensify over time. Results don't always kick in until well after a marketing program has been underway. When you shake things up by changing too soon or too often, you're wasting your money on each successive effort, which costs money to launch but never attains orbit.

This doesn't mean you should stick with a lousy ad campaign or promotion in the name of stability. Nor does it mean you should run the same ad or commercial forever. It simply means you should avoid the temptation to tamper during the critical germination period. Assuming you have a good marketing plan, stick with your plan once it's enacted.

WASTE NUMBER FOUR: MARKETING RESEARCH

Marketing research is like cholesterol: there's a good kind and a bad kind. The good kind of marketing research is based on what people are *actually doing*. Want to know how many boxes of Kellogg's Corn Flakes or cans of Quaker State motor oil or Detroit Tigers baseball caps people bought last year? Largely thanks to bar codes and computers, that information exists. And it's very accurate.

You can also learn a lot from *empirical observation* — simply noticing what people are actually doing. If there's one form of marketing research that's underutilized, it's plain old observation.

And it never hurts to survey your customers or clients with a *customer grading questionnaire*. Ask them to grade your product and service on a number of qualities. Some of your best ideas may actually come from your customers.

But the bad kind of marketing research — the kind that not only gobbles your budget but has the potential to destroy you — is *per-*

ceptual or *attitudinal* research. When you attempt to identify prevalent perceptions, attitudes, interests, and opinions, you're asking for trouble. Big trouble.

Not that there aren't some very competent research professionals that can produce a well-crafted, scientifically sound research project for you. Fielding mechanics and statistical reliability are not the problem. But we humans are very funny about answering questions about ourselves. In fact, we tend to provide highly inaccurate answers to such questions, because (*a*) we can't accurately recall things that aren't really important to us, (*b*) we're asked to give conscious thought and opinion to things that are primarily subconscious in nature, (*c*) we really want to get off the phone and the quickest way to do that is to give any random answer, (*d*) we really have no opinion but feel compelled to specify one anyway so as not appear uninformed or stupid, and (*e*) we want to give prestigious answers that make us look good.*

You know it's true: What people say they believe and do, and what people really believe and do, are two different things. You've seen evidence of this many times with friends or family members, haven't you?

Coca-Cola discovered the trappings of marketing research the hard way in 1985. That was the year, you'll recall, when they did away with the time-tested, highly successful "old" Coke — the then 99-year-old formula that became one of the most successful products in the world — and replaced it with the sweeter-tasting "new" Coke.

In April of that year, Coca-Cola's chairman Roberto Goizueta was a guest on CNN's "Moneyline" program. Host Lou Dobbs began by noting an opinion expressed by some Pepsi officials that Mr. Goizueta's decision to change the Coke formula was perhaps a foot-shooting move. To which Goizueta replied, "It's not a decision of mine. It's a decision made by the American consumers. Over 190,000

---

*The "garbology" studies of the 1970s illustrated this last point quite vividly. The researcher would, unbeknown to a homeowner, sift through that homeowner's trash can and find evidence of particular brand usage, empty Boone's Farm bottles, for example. Then the researcher would ring the doorbell and ask what kind of alcoholic beverage the homeowner drinks. Dom Perignon would be the answer.

consumers have told us . . . they prefer [the new taste of Coke] over the original Coke."

"Does it ever concern you," Dobbs prodded, "about your faith in consumer research . . . marketing research?"

"Well," Goizueta noted, "it's so overwhelming, so absolutely overwhelming, the results we have gotten . . . that we revere the consumer a lot more than we revere a 99-year-old formula, to be frank with you."

You know the outcome. After mounting public outcry and declining sales, Coca-Cola admitted its blunder and revived the "old" formula, renaming it Coca-Cola Classic. Meanwhile, the "new" formula — the one research said was overwhelming preferred by American consumers — accounts for a minute fraction of Coke's sales.

Television networks have long since been aware of the problems that can occur when you actually believe, and act upon, your marketing research. In research survey after research survey, people would say they prefer "documentaries" above all other types of television shows. So the networks would produce documentaries. And sure enough, they would end up as the least-watched shows time and time again. Research also indicates that most people object to shows with "too much sex and violence." Yet those shows usually end up at the top of the ratings. That's why you don't see many documentaries on the major networks. And that's why the majority of the characters on television today are either involved in slimy and tawdry sexual escapades week after week, or they carry a gun and shoot at people.

Why Do It?

If marketing research is so unreliable, why do so many companies spend so much time and money doing so much of it? Here's why:
- **Debate reduction.** When you have a menagerie of decision makers, debates can rage on and on. (Helen Slater to Michael J. Fox in *The Secret of My Success:* "There is no right or wrong, there is only opinion.") Research can be the arbiter than no one in the organization is willing to be.
- **Decision justification.** In a highly charged political environment, research may be your best ally. Heaven forbid you should

put your own judgment on the line by making a decision or mounting a cause without plenty of research to back you up. When the finger of guilt inevitably points your way one day, you can in turn point to the research, shrug your shoulders, and emerge virtually unscathed. Roberto Goizueta remained the chairman of Coca-Cola for a dozen more years after the New Coke fiasco (until his death in 1997).

- **Anxiety reduction.** Decisions can sometimes be tough to make. But when you've got a two-inch-thick research report pointing the way, it somehow becomes easier.
- **Competitive matching.** All of your competitors do it, so it must be worthwhile, right? Besides, you can't bear the thought that a competitor might just happen to stumble onto something, leaving you without so much as a line in the water.
- **It's addictive.** Research addicts feel they must have it monthly, weekly, daily, with every breath.

How Do You Kick The Research Habit?

- **Admit you don't need it.** The next time you're thinking of commissioning another project, think first about the five reasons for research I named above. Then ask yourself this question: If a situation demands debate reduction, decision justification, anxiety reduction, competition matching, or an addictive fix, doesn't the company or individual(s) in question have far greater problems than research could ever treat? Realize that the answer to any problems or opportunities that lie before you will not be found through marketing research — no more than water can be found with a diving rod.
- **Be skeptical of research findings.** The worst thing you can do is spend lots of money on perceptual or attitudinal research and then actually believe and act upon the findings. When you allow research to overrule your instincts and common sense, you're allowing bytemites (obsessive computer numbers crunchers) to run your life.

A research project from time to time won't hurt you as long as you learn to treat the findings with less than a grain of salt. The television networks spend millions on research each year, yet have learned to ignore most of it. (If research worked, they'd only air the shows that "tested well," and no show would ever fail.)

In radio, research reveals that the thing listeners complain about most is disc jockeys "talking over the music." So what do the disc jockeys do at the most successful, highest-rated stations? Talk over the music. (Talking over the instrumental beginning of songs creates excitement and stimulates emotions, which is desired by the subconscious. But listeners don't consciously know this; they don't know their brain actually likes the result of disc jockeys talking over the music.)

According to *Forbes*, Absolut vodka conducted a major research project in 1978 that concluded Absolut would fail in the United States because, among other things, the bottle didn't have a paper label and the neck was too small for bartenders to grab. How did Absolut react? Michel Roux, in charge at the time, simply threw the research out, noting "I just felt they didn't know what they were talking about." It didn't take long for Absolut to become the largest-selling imported vodka in the United States.

- **Save your money.** Once you learn to ignore research findings, the obvious question becomes: Why spend money on it in the first place? Save your money for the action-oriented tasks you'll be engaged in later.

WASTE NUMBER FIVE: CORE OVERKILL

Almost every marketer has a primary marketing target for each product or service. It's usually expressed in demographic terms, such as males aged 18 to 44 for audio/video equipment or females aged 24-49 for bedroom furniture.

Many marketers also like to compress their primary target into as thin or precise a demographic slice (called a "demo") as possible — compressing the male 18-44 demo down to males 25-34 with annual incomes in the $28,000-$55,000 range who own the own homes, for instance. A thinly defined demographic target is called a *core*. The more compressed or thin your core demo, the easier it is to cater to the common needs of core people. From a media-buying stand-point, it's also easier and cheaper to reach the core versus a much wider demo slice.

Core marketing, or "niche marketing" as it's sometimes called, has its advantages at times. But here's the rub: As a marketer continues to focus on his or her core over time, an ever-increasing percentage of the core-targeted marketing becomes ineffectual. In other words, your core becomes saturated. It's when core people are not going to buy any more of your product than they are already buying, no matter how many more marketing missiles you bombard them with (the old "point of diminishing returns"). Therefore, once you've maximized your core, a large percentage of your subsequent core-targeted marketing is useless, a waste of money.

Because so many marketers make the recurring mistake of allocating too much of the marketing budget to core-targeted activity, and because doing the opposite — targeting a much wider demo slice — can be extremely advantageous at times, I have devoted all of Chapter 11 to its further discussion.

WASTE NUMBER SIX: LARGE PRIZE CONTESTS WITHOUT MASS MARKET EXPOSURE

Large prizes can be useful at times. (Let's define large as anything over $1,000 in value.) They can be used to attract new consumers or customers who otherwise wouldn't make the effort to enter your contest and buy your product or service. But to make those large prizes pay off — to use them as bait to attract many new customers — you need mass market exposure of your contest. You need to reach lots of people who are not currently buying your product.

If, on the other hand, you do not arrange for mass market exposure of your contest, opting instead to reach only your existing customers (through, say, an entry blank attached to the product or an in-store display), save your money. Your existing customers simply do not need large prizes to motivate them to enter the contest or to buy more from you. For them, smaller prizes will be just as effective, and will cost you a whole lot less.

Here's the rule: Fuel a mass-marketed contest with large prizes (along with some smaller ones), and fuel a non-mass-marketed contest with small prizes exclusively.

PART 2

THE PSYCHOLOGY OF DEMAND

The term *demand* connotes a common desire among many people for a particular product or service. A handful of people who want a product does not constitute demand. To create demand, you must reach and affect a whole lot of people — thousands, tens of thousands, or millions.

But before we are ready to affect the masses, we must reduce demand down to its simplest form and understand how it works, as scientists might examine a single human cell to help determine how the whole body works.

People don't gather together as one multiperson unit and collectively decide whether or not to purchase your product or service. That decision is made on an individual basis, one human brain at a time. In this section, we'll discuss the psychology of demand — what goes on in the mind of the individual. You'll learn how to create *want* and *desire* in the minds of individuals, the first step in demand creation.

Chapter Five

What People *Really* Want

People want a lot of things: love, success, fun, health, security, companionship, money, you name it. Man is, indeed, a "wanting animal," and the true boundaries of man's want are limitless.

You needn't be concerned with the enormity of man's want, however. I've done the homework and boiled it all down for you. I've reduced the list down to four things. Four omnipotent wants that, either individually or in some combination, provide the powerful motivation behind the purchase of virtually any and all products and services. All you have to do is understand these four *power wants* and you will gain a tremendous advantage. This is the beginning of the demand-building process.

The power wants are inherent in all people, regardless of gender, race, age, nationality, social background, or economic status. They're also in effect all the time. That's what makes them so strong and potent. As we discuss each, think of ways you can use them in your own marketing program.

Note: Beginning now, and throughout the remainder of this book, I'll be using some specific, real-life ad campaigns as examples. Most are from large, nationally-known marketers. I use large-scale marketers as examples because that is what you are most likely to be familiar with. Please don't infer that the techniques under discussion are only for large-scale marketers. They're for you, regardless of the scale you're operating on.

POWER WANT NUMBER ONE: EMOTIONAL STIMULATION

Human beings crave emotional stimulation. Because when our emotions flow, it is a psychologically pleasing experience.

Mostly, people desire positive emotional feelings such as love, excitement, laughter, sexual attraction, security, etc. But the desire for emotional stimulation is so strong that people even enjoy negative emotions at times. In a strange way, negative emotions such as fear, sadness, loneliness, and anger can be enjoyable. That's why you see lines of people waiting to see horror movies or ride "death-defying" roller coasters. That's why they like sad songs and tear-jerking movies. Why is it your spouse or boyfriend or girlfriend will sometimes start an argument strictly for the sake of arguing (something we never do, of course)? Could it be that negative emotion is better than no emotion? Sometimes they want to stir you up just to get emotions flowing.

Think about how emotional stimulation relates to product purchases. Why do people purchase recorded music? The superficial reason is that they like a particular song or recording artist. The real reason is that certain music stimulates their emotions (positive or negative).

Why do people attend sporting events? To see their favorite team or player in action? Once again, the real underlying reason is that the whole event can be an emotionally stimulating experience.

Why do children love to get toys for Christmas and hate getting clothes? What do the toys do that the cloths do not?

Why do you take snapshots or video tape an event? Could it be because the pictures are great triggers that cause you to re-experience the emotion of the event again and again?

Provide Emotional Stimulation in Your Advertising

Okay, people want their emotions stimulated. So how does that happen? How do you, the marketer, induce or activate emotions?

Most often, your product or service itself won't be able to stimulate an emotion nearly as well as your advertising of the product or service. Put another way, your advertising, not your product or service, contains the emotion-stimulating force in most cases.

Take fast food, for example. A hamburger, fries, and soft drink are not inherently emotional things. Even consuming them isn't very emotional. Yet McDonald's advertisements show people in highly emotional states — high-school kids gathering to flirt with the opposite sex; mom, dad, and the kids coming to McDonald's as a family event; or McDonald's employees smiling, laughing, and dancing. The ads stimulate an emotion, to which the product or service is linked.

Build Psychological Links

The idea is to create psychological links between your product and a strong emotion. In your advertising, you first create an emotional situation, then link your product or service with it. The concept is really quite simple.

The next time you see a Coke or Pepsi commercial on television, look for the emotions that are depicted. You'll see people gathering, laughing, having the time of their lives. Or people of the opposite sex attracted to one another. Or athletes in a state of high exhilaration. And — you'll see cans of Coke or Pepsi at the same time. The ads stimulate an emotion, to which the product is linked.

My favorite example is Michelin. An automobile tire is not an emotionally-stimulating item. So Michelin links their tire with a very emotionally-stimulating item — a baby. When you see a baby sitting inside a Michelin tire, here's what happens: The baby activates your love emotion. Since you are seeing the tire at the same time, the love emotion and the tire are becoming linked in the subconscious part of your brain. See the ad a few times, and before long the love emotion gets linked to the tire in your brain. You now love Michelin tires! No wonder Michelin's sales have skyrocketed since the baby campaign began. (Before you cry "Wait a minute! That's manipulative!," consider this: Your brain wants emotional stimulation. By stimulating your love emotion with the cute baby, Michelin is doing what you want done to you, albeit on the subconscious level. Linking their tire is completely harmless. You're still in total control; you're free to buy any brand of tire you choose.)

How to Provide Emotional Stimulation in Your Advertising

Exactly how do you create an emotional situation and link your product/service to it in your advertising? Follow this three-step approach:

- **Step 1: Select the emotion(s) you wish to stimulate.** The four strongest positive emotions conducive to advertising are *excitement, love, laughter,* and *sexual attraction.*

  Some negative emotions are just as strong as these four positive emotions but are a lot trickier to use effectively. That's because people aren't always going to be paying close attention to your advertising, and they can inadvertently link your product with the negative emotion in their mind, even though you didn't intend for that to happen. For example, what might happen if your ad or commercial were to depict a person angry with himself for not purchasing your product or service? The casual receiver of that ad or commercial might easily link the negative emotion — anger — with your product or service in his mind.

  Let's discuss each of the four main positive emotions and see which might be best for you.

  The excitement emotion means the same thing as joy or fun. Think about the ways your ad or commercial can elicit feelings of joy or fun. Pontiac, for example, shows scenes of the car moving down water-slicked roadway, with music pumping and people interacting in the nighttime. The action is fast-paced and intense. The tag line, "We build excitement . . . Pontiac," spoon-feeds it to you.

  Although cigarette advertising is restricted these days, it is still a good example of linking a non-emotional object with emotion. Cigarette marketers like to link their products to excitement and/or sexual attraction. They show active people surfing, playing volleyball on the beach, racing automobiles, or rounding up cattle. Of course none of these exciting activities inherently have anything to do with smoking — but so what? No rule says linkage has to make logical sense.

Creating the love emotion is usually done by depicting interaction between family members. Because most people have strong feelings of love for members of their own family, it's easy to interpret. Hallmark, Kodak, McDonald's, and Coca-Cola have used family scenes in their advertising for years.

Sexual attraction is one of the most commonly used emotions in advertising because it's relatively easy to depict. You simply show two people in some state of attraction and link your product. Pepsi's done it with a commercial featuring Michael J. Fox. He meets his new female neighbor, to whom he is immediately attracted. She asks for a Pepsi, and he scrambles to get her one. Michelob's "The Night Belongs to Michelob" campaign shows members of the opposite sex interacting in a nightclub setting. Calvin Klein depicts sexual attraction in its clothing ads, as do Levi's and Guess. Hanes's "Gentlemen Prefer Hanes" campaign shows men ogling women wearing the product.

Laughter is stimulated through humor. The one drawback to humorous ads is that oftentimes the joke upstages the product. Try this experiment: Describe a humorous television commercial to someone and ask if they've seen it. When they say yes, then ask them to name the brand. Quite often, people can recall the commercial but not the brand. Sometimes, people recall the *wrong* brand. Energizer's ubiquitous bunny can be funny at times, but it turns out that a lot of people think it's a commercial for Duracell and not Energizer (Duracell used toy characters in their ads at one time).

An effective way to use humor is to make the name of the product the punchline. That way people can't help but get the brand name right. Kellogg's Nut 'N Honey cereal does just that, as the brand name is played upon ("nothin' honey") in a series of humorous vignettes.

- **Step 2: Depict people experiencing the emotion you want to stimulate.** You create an emotion, and cause your audience to feel it, by showing one or more people experiencing the emotion. Show the emotion in their faces and in their voices. (You don't necessarily need visual images to provide emotional stimulation. You can depict emotion quite well using voices, words, and music.)
- **Step 3: Depict the purchase of, or use of, your product or service.** After establishing the emotion, show people using your product. Or do it the other way around by showing people using your product, then experiencing the emotion as a result. Or show people experiencing the emotion while simultaneously using your product (implying a cause-and-effect relationship).

Honing Your Emotion-Creating Skills

Creating emotion-stimulating advertising is not always easy. It's more art than science, and it takes a good deal of practice and experience to become really good at it. You needn't become good at it, though. You can simply hire talented people to do it for you. These people can be found at advertising agencies and graphic or commercial production houses. But you do need an understanding of how it all works so you can guide the production people correctly.

Let's say you are one of those creative people, and you do want to hone your skills. If you want to become good at creating advertising that stimulates emotions, follow the advice of James Gartner, noted television commercial director.

Although a number of people are involved in the creation of a television commercial, it's the director who actually does what we've talked about — create the emotion and link the product or service. James Gartner has directed commercials for AT&T, Visa, IBM, FedEx, Coca-Cola, and Kodak, to name a few. His trademark is emotion-stimulating, sometimes heartwrenching, commercials.

"Surround yourself with good art, literature, film," he suggests. "Then dissect it. What is it about that particular piece that makes it stand out? In the case of a television commercial, play it back on your VCR 50 times. Notice the framing of each scene. The cutting. The pacing. The facial expressions. The dialogue. The lighting. The colors. Every element is important. It's the synergy of how all those elements are used. Pay attention to details. The smallest detail is often the difference between good and great. Remember, nothing communicates better than emotion in advertising."

POWER-WANT NUMBER TWO: PSYCHOLOGICAL RELIEF

We all live with problems, difficulties. The normal pressures and responsibilities of life produce feelings of discomfort such as tension, stress, anxiety, anger, despair, whatever. Yet our minds instinctively and subconsciously seek ways to relieve these uncomfortable or painful feelings. If your product helps reduce or relieve some of this psychological discomfort, people will want it.

Say, for example, you have the worst lawn in the neighborhood. You don't have the time to till the ground, plant grass seed, spread fertilizer, and nurture the lawn. But the pressure to "do something" about the problem is mounting. You feel the frustration and anxiety increasing as time goes on. Finally, when the psychological discomfort is great enough, you take action to relieve it. You decide to call a professional lawn care service. Once you hire it, the psychological discomfort is relieved.

How to Provide Psychological Relief

Providing psychological relief in your advertising is similar to providing emotional stimulation. You depict relief and link your product or service to it. If the link is clear and strong, your product is perceived as a *provider* or *facilitator* of the relief.

Here are the three steps in providing psychological relief:

- **Step 1: Choose a particular discomfort you would like to relieve.** Anxiety, frustration, disappointment, sadness, fright, desperation, embarrassment, anger, loneliness, and despair are a few possibilities. What type of discomfort would your typical consumer or customer experience with some regularity?
- **Step 2: Depict your product or service providing psychological relief.** There are two ways of doing this. One way is to es-

tablish the discomfort first, then introduce your product or service as the reliever. Napa Auto Parts shows a vehicle stuck on a railroad track with a train barreling down. Fright and despair. You feel the discomfort just looking at the scene, don't you? Luckily, the vehicle has Napa parts. It starts at the last second and the driver pulls away unharmed. Discomfort first, product (and the ensuing relief) second.

The other way is simply to establish the relief without ever establishing the prior discomfort. You imply a particular discomfort existed or would have existed prior to the product's use. Domino's Pizza shows a person pushing the buttons on the telephone (or, in a radio commercial, it uses the sounds of touch tones). As that occurs, the caller is depicted in a very happy state, as he is now relieved of having to worry about preparing dinner. Anxiety and hunger are the implied discomforts.

- **Step 3: Assume responsibility.** When you assume some responsibility for results, you're reassuring people that they will be relieved by no longer having to worry about the problem. Isn't this what the person is really buying anyway?

FedEx points out their competence in getting your valuable package to its destination the next day, without your having to worry about whether it will arrive on time or not. Orkin gives you a written guarantee, and tells you so in their advertising. If a pest reappears within a specified length of time after treatment, they'll come back and fix the problem at no charge. Midas will replace your new muffler free for as long as you own the vehicle. Craftsman tools are guaranteed for life. If one ever breaks, bring it back to Sears and they'll replace it free of charge. Many retailers have a no-questions-asked return policy.

Remember, people are buying psychological relief. When they buy your product or service, they should be relieved of having to worry about the problem from that point forward. (Not that your product or service is expected to eradicate all of life's ills. Reasonable parameters, placing limits on the responsibility you assume, should apply.)

Link Relief to the Purchase Decision

You may have noticed that in many cases, you can depict psychological relief as occurring at the time of the purchase decision rather than when the product is actually used. Domino's shows a person experiencing relief when ordering the pizza, not necessarily having to wait until eating the pizza to experience relief. When you hired the lawn care company, didn't you feel relief right after making the call? You don't have to wait until they begin or even complete the job to feel relief, do you?

When someone hires me to speak at their convention, conference, or meeting, they feel relief at the time they hire me, which may be many months before I actually show up to speak. I play up this benefit in my marketing materials, pointing out that when you hire Rick Ott you no longer have to worry about finding an entertaining and relevant speaker — that burden has been lifted from your shoulders the second you choose Rick Ott.

When you depict psychological relief occurring at the time the purchase decision is made, you strengthen the link between relief and your product or service. You increase your impact appreciably.

POWER-WANT NUMBER THREE: HIGHER STATUS

From the time humans first walked on Earth up to the present day, every human society has ranked its members by some stated or implied class structure. From hunting and gathering times to the feudal days of serf, king, and queen, to modern times, every society has been organized by some type of social class structure. (Animals and insects operate the same way, too.) Social scientists have long been interested in the phenomenon, and the number of studies that have been done on the subject could fill the room you're occupying right now.

But all you have to know is this: People seek to gain higher social status; to rise in rank. The tendency to crave higher status is instinctive and normal, and is averted only when a person consciously chooses otherwise. (Even some religious orders that denounce money and other material possessions as measures of social stature are still subject to their own internal pecking order based on whatever measures they've chosen.)

Some people are, of course, more status-conscious than others, but only to an insignificant degree. What often appear to be differences in status consciousness are actually differences in status *circles*, not consciousness. In other words, your neighbor may not wear Armani suits or drive a Mercedes, but that doesn't mean he's oblivious to status. It just means he's not in the same circle as those who use Armani and Mercedes to display status. Perhaps an Orvis fishing rod and Ford Explorer are considered status symbols in his circle.

We naturally seek to rise in status because it feels good when we gain respect and admiration in the eyes of people important to us. (If we dissect status, we find respect and admiration as its primary components.) The desire for respect and admiration is ubiquitous and transcends all man-made boundaries.

Children quickly learn about status as they begin interacting with other kids. The Boy Scouts and Girl Scouts have a formal ranking structure that teaches the relative value of each rank and rewards hard work with raises in rank. Even renegade street gangs have status structures. Many gang wars are over nothing more than status supremacy. In high school we learn quickly that sophomores are peons, juniors are respectable, and seniors are almighty. I can still remember when sophomore year was finally over and I became a junior; I felt as though I'd been instantly pulled out of the depths of desolation and anointed with honor. Now a new crop of lowly sophomores can wallow in the quagmire and adulate us exalted juniors! Status can be most exhilarating.

How People Attain Higher Status

The way people gain higher status is to *associate* themselves with things that provide higher status, and *disassociate* with things that provide lower status.

For example, people buy and wear designer clothes because of the status association. A designer label on your clothes is like a sign on your back that says "I'm in a high, respectable class."

Automobiles are strong status symbols. Remember when every

30-year-old yuppie in the 1980s felt compelled to drive a BMW or Mercedes? He or she had to show others in their circle that they'd "made it," and thus deserved respect and admiration.

Why do people naturally gravitate toward celebrities? Celebrities are, in general, perceived to be of high status. (There's nothing like media exposure to transform commoners into royalty.) When people ask for an autograph or to have their picture taken with a celebrity, they're really trying to gain a status rise for themselves by the association.

Speaking of celebrities, they too crave higher status. Performers in concert hate appearing first on the bill, since "opening" is low status. "Headlining," playing last on the bill, is higher status. If tradition dictated just the opposite, that higher status went to those that appeared first, performers would all want to be the opening act.

In sports, it is the opposite. Think about how many professional athletes strive to be a "starter" (starting quarterback, starting pitcher, or simply in the starting lineup). Somewhere along the line, prestige became associated with starting, so athletes aspire to start.

Once status symbols are established, can they be changed? All it would take is for one professional football team to pay a backup quarterback as much or more than it pays the starting quarterback, and the prestige associated with the backup position would be established. (It would also help to do away with the term "backup" and replace it with "ace reliever," or "closer," as is done in baseball.)

In fact, this is exactly what happened in baseball. Prior to 1984, a relief pitcher was considered lower status than a starting pitcher. But in '84, the Atlanta Braves signed "ace reliever" Bruce Sutter to a six-year, $9.6 million contract — making Sutter the highest-paid pitcher in baseball at the time. Since then, it's been just as prestigious to be a reliever or closer as it is to be a starter.

People also disassociate with people and things they perceive as low status. In every school, there are always one or two kids that no other kids will have anything to do with. These outcasts may understandably, though mistakenly, conclude that no one likes them, or that there's something wrong with them. But that has nothing to do with it. The reason they lack peer acceptance is that, for whatever reason, they're considered to be of low status, and others feel compelled to disassociate. Every once in a while an outcast will do something that causes others to embrace him. Did the outcast suddenly change his personality or become another person? No. He just changed his status.

Products and services have perceived levels of status, which can vary depending on social circles. Why is it some people have no trouble buying certain items of clothing at Kmart, yet these same people would die before admitting that's where their clothes came from? In some circles, Kmart is considered low status; in other circles it's just fine. (Kmart shouldn't be singled out in this regard. Wal-Mart, Target, or any other discount retailer represents the same low degree of status to some.) That's why Kmart hired Jaclyn Smith as a spokesperson and put her name on a line of clothing — and Wal-Mart did the same with Kathie Lee Gifford — to raise the level of perceived status in its target market.

Watch what people say and do with regard to disassociation. When someone expresses a dislike for a particular product or service, it can quite often be traced directly back to a desire to disassociate based on a lack of perceived status. ("I hate this dress!," she said.) However, when questioned, they will always give a logical-sounding reason for their dislike; no one likes to consciously admit status is the underlying factor. ("It's too loose-fitting . . . and it doesn't go with my shoes.")

How to Provide Status

When you link your product or service to something or someone that represents a certain level of status, some of that status will transfer or rub off onto your product or service.

There are a number of ways to link your product or service with some level of status, but here are the most potent:

- **Higher Price.** In a capitalist society, money is the single most significant measure of status (rightly or wrongly). That being the case, people oftentimes want to purchase expensive things as a display of status.

    People brag about living in an expensive house, in an expensive neighborhood. They want you to see their expensive watch, jewelry, or clothes. They talk about the expensive school they're sending their kids to, the high-dollar law firm they're using, or the prestigious consulting firm they've hired. And, of course, they really want you to salivate over their car. A few years ago a professional speaker colleague adamantly insisted the four of us, who were planning on having dinner together, ride in his car from the hotel to the restaurant. He was so determined to drive that we acquiesced and got in his brand new, top-of-the-line Mercedes. Whereupon he spent ten minutes showing us every whistle and bell imaginable on that car, before finally driving the 100 or so yards from the hotel to the restaurant.

Cuisinart food processors sell for considerably more than their counterparts made by Waring or Oster. Cuisinart made an interesting observation a while back. People don't put their food processors away, out of sight, when they're not using them. They keep them sitting on the kitchen counter. Anytime you have a product or service that the buyer "displays" in some way, you have an opportunity to use status to your advantage. By charging a comparatively high price for its product, Cuisinart turned its food processor into a status symbol.

Remember, if people didn't willingly pay high prices for things, Rolex would never sell a watch, Waterford would never sell a crystal goblet, Starbucks would never sell a cup of coffee, Harley-Davidson would never sell a motorcycle, and FedEx would never deliver a package, just to name a few examples.

No, a high price strategy isn't for every marketer. Many marketers do well with a low price strategy. But beware — playing the low price game is the toughest game in town, and you'd better be amongst the best of the best if you're going to win at that game. The toughest kid in the neighborhood eventually runs across someone a little bit tougher. There's always another marketer somewhere willing and able to undercut your price. When you play the low price game, the playground is laden with quicksand. Vulnerability reigns, and you can spend so much time looking over your shoulder you lose sight of where you're going.

But you say your product or service is so common you can't realistically raise the price and still be competitive? That may be true if your product is a commodity item, where there are few perceived differences among brands. Then again, if you've created some significant product/service, container, or distribution differences, you may pull your product out of the commodity hole. After all, there's nothing more common in the world than water. Most of it doesn't even have a brand name. Yet Perrier, Evian, Deer Park, Aquafila, and others bottle it and sell it for around 30 times more than what it costs you for the same amount of tap water from the kitchen sink. (And it turns out some brands of bottled water are nothing more than plain old tap water!)

- **Celebrity endorsements.** Celebrities exude status. That's why you see so many products and services endorsed by celebrities. A celebrity can give a product instant status.

   Celebrities must have quite an allure to command the endorsement fees they do. Pepsi once paid Michael Jackson $15 million to appear in two Pepsi television commercials (he didn't even hold up a can). Pepsi also paid Madonna $5 million to appear in one commercial (which aired only once). And athletes often make much more money through product endorsements than they do through their regular salary or winnings.

   Can't afford to pay a big-name celebrity to endorse your small business? Try hiring local celebrities, such as radio personalities. Or, create celebrity status for yourself. Car dealers have been doing it for years. I'll bet there's at least one car dealer in your home town that appears in the media spotlight so much he's more well-known than the mayor.

- **Status depiction.** Simply depict people in a relatively high-status situation using your product or service.

   Grey Poupon does it by showing affluent people going out of their way to ask for the mustard. Johnnie Walker Black Label shows two neighbors standing outside their mansions discussing the product. Tasters Choice coffee shows a classy woman borrowing the product from a neighbor who informs her that "Tasters Choice is a very sophisticated coffee."

   As I've pointed out, status is relative. The way you depict status in your marketing depends on the way status is determined in the circle(s) you're targeting. In some circles, driving an Oldsmobile is high status; in other circles it's low status. In some circles, drinking Budweiser is high status; in other circles not.

Here's the key: Depict status at one or two levels higher than that of your target consumer. People instinctively seek to rise in status, so they associate with products and services that pull them up. A few years ago Maybelline cosmetics made the observation that the majority of women who purchase their products do not look like high fashion models. So they decided to use ordinary, "average looking women" in their ads, figuring that woman would better relate to someone similar to themselves. Sales plummeted. Why, after all, would someone want to associate with a product that kept them on the same level they're already on? People want to rise in status, not stay level. When Maybelline went back to the glamourous women in their ads, sales rebounded.

Want to appeal to men? Show an under-35-year-old, well-built, virile-looking male using the product, and men 40 and up, who look nothing like the man in the ad, will buy it.

Want to appeal to teens? The most status thing in their world is to be adult. Say your product is for adults, and show males and females in their 20s in your ads. Teens want adult status, and they'll latch onto things that offer it. (Which is why teen smoking will always exist. As long as smoking is an adult activity, teens will want to be seen doing it.)

POWER-WANT NUMBER FOUR: WHAT OTHERS WANT

People want what other people want. That's because the value you and I place on things is largely influenced by the value other people place on those things.

The best example of this occurs every day in the stock market. If you see the stock of X Company rising . . . rising . . . rising . . . you value it more yourself. You may even develop a strong desire to purchase that stock. But if X Company stock starts to fall . . . and fall . . . and fall, you will find it increasingly unattractive. You may even sell your shares. Why hang onto a stock that other people don't value highly?, you reason. What good is it if other people don't want it? (The scenario I've just described is, incidently, a great way to lose money in the market. If you want to make money in the stock market, you have to do the opposite of human nature and buy when a stock is low in price — when others don't value it so much.)

Teens learn how their own value is determined in the dating market. "Playing hard to get," which is a way of indicating you're valued highly by others, somehow results in greater desire on the part of another to date you. Come to think of it, adults do the same thing. If someone began taking a more-than-passing interest in your husband or wife, would you suddenly develop a heightened appreciation for your spouse? Would you find yourself reacting in a way that drew your spouse's attention to you?

Say a big-time boxing match, auto race, or tennis match is scheduled to take place in your city. People all over the country are converging on your hometown — reporters, fans, the works. The excitement level gets higher as the even draws closer. It seems everyone is talking about the event, and expressing a desire to attend. People are clamoring to get the limited number of tickets available. Most of the people you know don't have tickets but wish they could somehow get hold of one or two. Suddenly, and old acquaintance pops out of the shadows and offers you a pair. He'll sell you two tickets at the printed price, the only stipulation being that you don't resell them. Would you buy the tickets?

Of course you would, even if you had no real interest in the event. You've seen how valuable those tickets are, and you're not about to let them slip through your hands. You place a high value on those tickets, not because you're really interested in boxing, auto racing, or tennis, but because so many other people are. (And perhaps many of them are also interested for the same reason. Demand can be very contagious at times.)

Now let's look at the same situation with only one slight difference: same event, same stakes, same venue, same everything except no reporters, no crowds of people swarming to get tickets. In fact, no one you know is even talking about the event. When it does come up in conversation, people shrug and sight "other plans" that get in the way of their attending. Plenty of tickets are available, and your shadowy friend calls with his two-ticket offer. Would you buy the tickets? Evidently no one else wants the tickets, so why should you? If you're like most people, you'd pass on the tickets this time.

People line up to see certain movies, not deterred by the long lines and thick crowds (in fact, the throng of people attracts others). When the movie *Titanic* came out in the Fall of 1997, people flocked to theatres in droves, making *Titanic* one of the all-time blockbuster hits. Yet it was based on an old story (in fact, there were numerous other Titanic movies before), everyone knew how it was going to end, and everyone knew they were going to see people suffering as the ship went down (another example of the desire for emotional stimulation, even when the emotion is negative). Why would anyone want to see such a movie? Because everyone else is seeing it, that's why.

Here's an experiment you can try sometime. Ask someone to evaluate a party he attended recently. A simple "How was the such-and-such party?" is all you need to ask. Ninety-five percent of the time, the person answering will base his opinion strictly on the number of people that showed up. If the place was jammed, the party was "great!" If few people attended, the party "sucked." If the answerer based his evaluation on anything other than the number of people there, you can bet it was his party.

How to Link Your Product or Service with Want

The idea is to portray your product or service as wanted by many people. You can do that by implying a state of existing demand.

The owner of a new restaurant asked her employees to park their cars in front, as close to the door as possible, so that people driving by got the impression it was busy.

My dentist told me how he linked himself with want when he first began his practice years ago. He instructed his receptionist to schedule appointments overlapping each other on the same day so patients would see one another coming and going. Even though he had only a few patients at first, it appeared he was busy.

Six months after Subway Sandwiches opened in 1965, it was in financial trouble, close to ruin. What did the owners do? Why, they expanded, of course. Subway opened a second store and promoted it with flyers thanking everyone for making the first one "so successful." Soon the illusion of demand produced real demand.

An attorney I know instructed his receptionist to always say he was either "in court" or "meeting with a client" whenever anyone called. This guy must be pretty good if he's always busy with clients, right? Actually he was busy giving his dartboard a good workout half the time. But what would people think if he actually came on the phone right when they called? They'd get the impression he wasn't in demand — wasn't desired or valued by lots of other people — hardly the type of attorney anyone would want to hire.

SUMMARY

What people really want, and expect to attain by purchasing something, is seldom obvious (even to the buyer). As you may have noticed, the power-wants — the motivating forces behind all purchase decisions — are deeply subconscious. Even you and I, as consumers, are seldom aware of the real reasons why we want and buy certain things (unless we consciously analyze ourselves based on the material in this chapter). As a matter of fact, people won't even admit their actions are based on a desire for the four things we've discussed, even when you bring it to their attention!

Remember, the idea is to link your product or service with one or more of the power-wants: emotional stimulation, psychological relief, higher status, and what others want. The stronger the link, the more people will want your product or service.

POWER-WANT CHECKLIST

Each time you prepare an ad or commercial, a promotion or contest, run it through the following series of questions. You may not be able to use all of the power-wants all of the time, but this checklist will keep you from inadvertently forgetting one that may make the difference between minor and major results.

1. Are you stimulating an emotion in your photos, speech, or written copy? What emotion(s) are you stimulating?

2. Are you offering psychological relief? What discomfort(s) are you relieving? Are you taking some responsibility so the buyer can feel he no longer has to worry about the situation once he purchases your product or service?

3. Is your product or service connoting a particular level of status? Is the level of status you connote at least one notch higher than that of your target consumer? When they buy, use, or display your product, do they feel increased respect and admiration?

4. Are you implying an existing, strong degree of demand? Are you letting people know, either blatantly or subtly, that many others value your product or service highly?

Chapter Six

Magnetizing Your Marketing

Whenever I ask people to name a few qualities or attributes of good marketing, I get answers like these: creative, memorable, penetrating, clever, different, grabbing, and persuasive. I'm sure you can add one or two more to the list.

Next question: If you want your marketing to have some of these desirable qualities, how do you go about getting them? In other words, just what makes your marketing penetrating, memorable, or persuasive? Do you know exactly how to get these qualities, or do you just do your best and hope they somehow appear?

There are four main factors that determine the effectiveness of any marketing program. I call them the *power-attractors*. When you make good use of one or more of the power-attractors, your marketing will be penetrating, memorable, persuasive, and more. By proper application of the power-attractors, you will magnetize your marketing, greatly enhancing your product's attractiveness.

DIFFERENCES FROM POWER-WANTS

There are three important differences between the power-attractors and the power-wants we discussed in the previous chapter. First, unlike the power-wants, which are deeply imbedded in the subconscious, the power-attractors are much closer to the surface. People are usually consciously aware of the power-attractors and have no problem acknowledging their existence.

Second, whereas the power-wants are in people, the power-attractors are primarily in your product or service. To be more accurate, the power-attractors are attributes of your product or of the ways your product is marketed.

Third, the power-wants are activated mainly through advertising. The power-attractors are expressed through advertising as well, but also through other areas of marketing such as your product/service differences and container differences.

POWER-ATTRACTOR NUMBER ONE: FAMILIARITY

Have you ever asked a person what she thinks of a particular product or service, only to get the answer "Never heard of it"? Essentially, the other person is implying that the product or service or company in question is undesirable or of dubious value. And by what measure? Lack of familiarity.

Conversely, people are naturally attracted to that with which they are most familiar. There are two reasons why this is true:

- **The brain likes to take the easy route.** Your brain works by electrical impulse, just like your computer, clock radio, toaster, or anything else that runs on electricity. And electricity takes the shortest, least resistant route available. With the unfamiliar, the brain first has to make sense of it, evaluate it on some good/bad scale, and file it away in memory. But the brain doesn't have to spend any time or energy processing something with which it is already familiar. So it prefers the familiar over the unfamiliar. Make sense?
- **Familiarity represents less risk.** Most people harbor a natural aversion to risk most of the time. In fact, sometimes we'll stick

with something we don't even like, just because it's familiar (and avoid possibly improving things because that might require venturing into unfamiliar territory.)

Familiarity Dominates

But aren't there times when we're attracted to the unfamiliar? Aren't there times when a person wants to assume some risk? After all, people want to try new restaurants, see new movies, meet new people, and go on African safaris at times, don't they? Yes, but it takes a conscious effort to seek newness and override our fears, whereas it takes no conscious effort to gravitate toward the familiar. Familiarity, primarily governed by instinctive, subconscious desire, dominates most of the time.

Breaking Down the Instinct Barrier

Familiarity also helps break down what I call the *instinct barrier.* Say you suddenly become aware of a particular product or service. You are unfamiliar with it, yet you are asked to make the purchase decision quickly, shortly after your first exposure to it. Unless you consciously override it, your brain will go into a defensive mode and produce the instinct barrier. Subconsciously, you will choose the more familiar route, which is to do without the product or buy a more familiar brand. In other words, your subconscious mind needs more information — increased familiarity — with the product before it chooses to purchase.

Do you ever find yourself feeling somewhat uncomfortable and hesitant at the time of a purchase decision? That's the instinct barrier. It's telling you to gather more information — become more familiar with the product, service, company, or seller — before deciding to buy.

How to Build Familiarity

Here are the keys to establishing familiarity:
   • **Repeat, repeat, repeat.** There is almost no practical limit to the number of times your logo or name should appear in your

newspaper and magazine ads, in your radio and television commercials, at your promotional events, and in your stores or office.

I once pointed out to a department store executive that if a person were to be blindfolded and taken to his (the executive's) department store, and the blindfold removed in the middle of the men's clothing department, the person could look around all he wanted and still have no idea what store he was in. The store's logo was simply nowhere in sight. "But people don't enter our store blindfolded," he replied. He missed the point. Identifying yourself to those unaware is only part of your objective. Establishing and maintaining familiarity, which comes from repeated exposure to your logo, are the real keys.

- **Use multiple media.** Seeing or hearing from different sources is stronger than seeing or hearing from the same source.
- **A greater number of smaller-sized impressions is more effective than a lesser number of larger-sized impressions.** (Making something "smaller-sized" means using shorter-length commercials or smaller ad sizes.)

Here's an illustration of how familiarity is created through numerous impressions. Let's say you're a sales clerk at a clothing store. On Monday a new customer you've never seen before walks in. We'll call her Jody. She spends 25 minutes in your store, makes a purchase, and leaves. Also on Monday, another customer you've never seen before enters. His name is Bob. He spends five minutes in the store, purchases, and leaves. On Tuesday, Bob returns. He spends another five minutes in your store, purchases, and leaves. On Wednesday, Bob returns again for five minutes before purchasing and leaving. He does the same thing Thursday and Friday.

Jody spent 25 minutes in your store this week, and so has Bob. But whom are you most familiar with, Jody or Bob? Notice that you were exposed to each for the same length of time, 25 minutes. But Bob's numerous visits, albeit for shorter lengths of time, increased his familiarity level significantly. If Bob kept this up, it wouldn't be long before you'd think of him as a good friend and added him to your Christmas list.

Do savvy salespeople make a client visit and take care of

three items at once, or do they make three separate visits, with one agenda item each? If they want the client to develop familiarity with them, to forge a bond, they do the latter.

Marketing works the same way. Going with a larger number of smaller-sized ads or shorter-length commercials can increase your effectiveness, and stretch your budget. That's why 15-second television commercials have replaced 30-second commercials as the norm. Even if you have the budget to buy full-page ads or 60-second commercials, you should consider downsizing and running more of them instead. (There are exceptions. Thirty-minute infomercials work better than 30-second infomercials.)

- **Use testimonials with familiar people.** You can often establish familiarity more quickly if you use a testimonial from someone with whom the public is already familiar. These third-party endorsers act as conduits for the transfer of familiarity from the endorser to your product, service, or company.

POWER-ATTRACTOR NUMBER TWO: RESTRAINT

Restraint is the practical application of the "less is more" theory. In marketing, there are many instances when the less availability, time, and space you use, the more attractive your product or service becomes. Let's examine those three dimensions: *availability restraint, time restraint,* and *space restraint.*

Availability Restraint

Restraining availability can increase the perceived value of your product or service. After all, rare things are more valuable than common things.

What could be more limited in quantity than an art object? In most cases, the rareness of a one-of-a-kind painting or sculpture contributes to its value and demand.

Have you ever seen the print ads for various items from The Franklin Mint? It markets decorative "art" objects such as knives, rings, porcelain cats, swords, old western badges, and goblets. Each of these items is "minted" and "issued" by The Franklin Mint to those who either "subscribe" or "commission" the sale. In most cases, the items are produced in limited quantities.

You can actually create a feeding frenzy by restraining supply on the front end. Ever seen people standing in line for hours (days?) to buy tickets to some event? They won't let you buy the tickets until a specified day and time . . . and the tougher it is to get those tickets, the more you want them!

Limiting your own personal availability can increase your demand. As I mentioned earlier, teens learn that playing "hard to get" somehow results in attracting another person. And you know that interest in you as an employee rises in direct proportion to outside interest in you from another company. Hey, there's only one you, and you can exploit that by placing tighter restraints on your availability.

Which doctor would you choose, one who was available on a moment's notice or one requiring a five-week advance booking? You might want to see a doctor as soon as possible, but you'd probably have a lot more confidence in the busy one. Actors know that nothing contributes more to their demand than their unavailability. It's the same with attorneys and consultants. And let's not forget the job candidate. It's always easier to get a job when you already have one.

When MTV banned Madonna's "Justify My Love" video, guess what happened? Radio stations around the country arranged private showings, and people flocked to attend. It became the most requested video on the Video Jukebox cable channel. Music stores reported record-breaking sales of the video within days of the MTV banning.

I'm trying to figure out a way to get this book banned. Nothing, it seems, helps sell a book more than a well-publicized banning. Sometimes the mere mention of limited availability, without its actually occurring, is all you need. Victor Ostrovsky's book *By Way of Deception* shot to the top of the best-seller lists right after the Israeli government asked that it be banned, though no such ban ever occurred.

Availability is one thing, access another. By limiting availability, you increase perceived value and subsequent demand. All that happens *before* the purchase. *After* the purchase, the buyer should be able to get access to the item purchased fairly quickly. Some retailers, for example, are open limited hours such as weekends only. But once there, you get the item you want without delay.

Marketers that fail to provide quick access to an item purchased are creating trouble for themselves. Take the catalog showrooms, for example. Ever buy something from Service Merchandise or the old Best Products (not to be confused with Best Buy)? Once I decided to buy a clock radio at Best Products, I had to fill out an Order Form. My name, address, phone number, and "product number," whatever that is. Then I walked over to the Customer Service counter and waited for a minute or two until someone took my Order Form and entered it into the computer. "Yeah, we got it in stock," she informs me, adding "it'll be ready at Customer Pick-Up in twelve minutes." Twelve minutes?!? What am I supposed to do for twelve minutes? Eleven, ten, nine . . . I'm wandering around, daydreaming, passing the time . . . until I finally see my clock radio creeping down a conveyor belt and lodging itself amongst half-a-dozen other boxes. Another minute or so and someone picks it up, calls my name, and hands it to me. Finally, I'm holding the item . . . and now I have to move to the Check Out counter, where I wait in line for another five minutes! I could have been in and out of Wal-Mart five times in the time it took to work my way through the Best Products maze. No wonder Best Products filed for bankruptcy and eventually shut down all together.

Restrict availability to make your product or service more attractive. But once someone buys it, make sure he or she gets quick access.

Time Restraint

When you restrict time, you're essentially saying to the consumer, "We are not here whenever you need us. We're here for a limited time only, after which we will be gone and you will have lost out if you don't act now."

Ever pass on the opportunity to marry someone, then find out some time later that the person you rejected got married? How did it feel? Did you feel tinges of regret or loss? You could have had that person . . . you let them go . . . someone else snagged them . . . and now they're unavailable. Even if you made the right decision, it still feels lousy, doesn't it?

People want to avoid feeling that they "lost out" on an opportunity. When you introduce a time restraint, you can cause people to buy.

No one did that better than George Bush during the 1988 presidential race. In the middle of the second broadcast debate between Bush and Michael Dukakis, Bush was asked if he would agree to another (third) debate. The studio audience applauded the question, reinforcing the prevailing sentiment that debates are good and that every self-respecting, image-conscious politician automatically yearns to engage in them. Then Bush stunned everyone by replying, "No. I will not agree to another debate." After a couple seconds of shocked silence, the audience burst out in thunderous applause. Bush's unexpected restriction of his time may have indeed tipped the scales in his favor at that point.

Everyone loved the Lone Ranger. He breezed into town, saved the day, and got out before anyone had the chance to think less of him. If you followed him back to his favorite rock, or wherever he lived, and had to watch him do his laundry, cook rabbit stew, and complain about his aching back, would his mystique have dwindled any? The Lone Ranger was a master of time restraint, knowing that his absence made him all the more attractive.

Disney restrains the time period in which their home videos can be purchased, often pulling them off the market for years at a time. In other words, you'd better buy a copy now, while you've got the chance, because after next week they're going to be gone and you're going to be out of luck! Try explaining that to your screaming six-year-old.

In the record business, exposure of new songs on radio stations or music-oriented television shows or cable channels is essential. Record companies put a lot of effort into promoting their material to the radio and television programming people who decide what songs to air.

So how does a record company virtually guarantee itself a ton of airplay with a minimal effort? By turning the tables and introducing a time restraint. When a relatively hot artist releases a new album, the record company will sometimes restrict airplay by declaring an "official release date," before which the song or album "may not be played" on air. What happens when you tell radio people they can't play a song or album? They scramble to get hold of it and play it. They often obtain advance copies leaked from mysterious, unnamed sources. They get it on the air as soon as possible — before the release date — so as to beat competing stations and subsequently brag that they were the first station to air it. Sometimes the record company will issue a cease-and-desist order (yes, they are asking the stations not to air the songs), or threaten a law suit (which never really happens, or course). At any rate, by simply placing a time restraint on the front end (as opposed to a back-end time restraint which cuts off availability at some point), the record company gets the mass exposure and on-air hype it covets.

Space Restraint

If you give people too much physical space, they'll get a sense there's something wrong, and they'll be repelled. Restrict the amount of physical space, and people will become attracted. Sound strange? Well, consider this:

You and your friends, headed for an exciting night on the town, narrow your choice of nightclubs down to two. The first place is packed with people by 9 P.M. when you arrive. In fact, people are standing in line to get in. The second nightclub across the street has no line to get in and plenty of empty space inside. Which place do you choose?

Most people would prefer the first place, since it appears to be where the action is. The second place appears actionless, and therefore less desirable.

Now here's the interesting part. Both nightclubs had the exact same number of people, 200, in attendance when you checked them out. Why, then, did the first place appear to be happening and the second place dead? Because the first place was physically smaller and held only 200 people; it appeared packed. The second place held 600 people and it appeared practically empty. Remember power-want number four? People want what others want. When you restrain the physical space, you can create that condition.

Think about perfume or cologne. I'm sure you've noticed that the most expensive and desirable brands give you very little of the actual product in the bottle. By restricting the physical space — designing the bottle to hold very little liquid — the manufacturer raises its attractiveness.

In years past, physically larger products used to be more attractive than smaller products. The proliferation of the microchip has altered people's perceptions in recent years, however. With computers, telephones, and other electronic gadgets getting more powerful as they get smaller, the perceived relationship between size and value — in other areas as well as in electronics — has become inversely related. In fact, small can be prestigious. The person with the smallest digital phone is the coolest, it seems.

Can you increase your product's attractiveness by restraining space in some way? Think creatively and the answer may come to you.

POWER-ATTRACTOR NUMBER THREE: DISTANCE/PROXIMITY

This power-attractor has to do with the geographic origin of your product or service.

Distance

In some cases, the farther away from the potential buyer's home town your product's perceived origin, the more attractive it becomes. Which vase would you feel better about displaying in you home, the one you brought back from Mexico, or the one you bought at the discount store down the street?

If you had a choice of two brands of beer, one brewed near your hometown and the other brewed halfway across the country, which would you choose? Before Coors went national, people in parts of the country in which Coors was unavailable used to treat it like some rare delicacy. They'd bring it back from a Denver vacation or have it shipped to them by friends. To some, even a beer from across the country isn't good enough. They prefer an imported beer, something brewed in Mexico, Canada, or Germany.

The word *imported* attached to some items (or simply implied) can make them immediately more attractive. Häagen-Dazs ice cream is a domestic brand. In fact, it's been around since the 1960s, which makes it a traditional domestic brand. But its name makes it sound imported, and many people mistakenly believe that it is.

Although I'm based in Richmond, Virginia, most of my clients are in other cities, other states. Why? Because in the speaking, seminar, consulting business, the farther we travel to get to a client, the more valuable our advice and wisdom is perceived to be.

Proximity

In other cases, the closer your product's origin to where it is purchased or consumed, the more attractive it is.

A politician is going to have a very difficult time winning election if he or she hasn't spent many years living in the jurisdiction in which they seek office. No community wants an "outsider" to show up and tell them how to live or claim to be familiar with their interests.

Proximity is everything when it comes to sports. People naturally root for the team closest to them, or the team they once lived near. In fact, people can become very emotional and expressive with regard to their favorite team. (Don't you wish people would scream and cheer as loud about your brand or company?)

The cities of Brunswick, Virginia and Brunswick, Georgia are battling one another over the right to claim they invented brunswick stew. People in the respective cities brag about the stew made in their town, and denigrate the stew made in the other.

Some services are perceived to be more valuable when the provider is of nearby origin. Would you call a plumber that lived hundreds of miles away, or one that lived in your town? Who would you trust to pave your driveway, a company based only a few miles away or one that came from who-knows-where? And what attorney would you want, the one who lives in the community in which the trial is taking place or the one from far away?

Determine whether distance or proximity is a positive attribute of your particular product, service, or business. Then play it up in your advertising.

POWER-ATTRACTOR NUMBER FOUR: A GOOD DEAL

I mentioned in the previous chapter that people want things that cost a lot of money because expensive things provide status. People have no problem spending money for expensive things, as long as they feel they're getting their money's worth.

And what determines if a person feels they're getting their "money's worth"? The universal answer: a good deal. While there are countless variables that affect how a person perceives your product or service, the one thing that does not vary is a good deal. People always want a good deal, meaning they appreciate — even crave — getting an expensive thing for less than the going price.

The Expensive-Deal Strategy

Let's review for a moment how a high price contributes to attractiveness. A $600 suit is more desirable than a $200 suit, wouldn't you say? A $36,000 car is more desirable than a $16,000 car. A $35 bottle of perfume is more desirable than a $7 bottle (even when you get four times as much of the cheaper stuff). An accounting firm that charges $150 an hour is more desirable than one that charges $50 an hour.

Likewise, the word "expensive" often works for you. People are proud of the fact that they drive an expensive car, that they eat in expensive restaurants, that they stay in expensive hotels, that they wear expensive clothes, that they received an expensive gift on Valentine's Day, and that they have an expensive law firm on their case. (Be careful how you use the work "inexpensive." Don't assume that something inexpensive is automatically attractive.)

Now let's examine how a high price can work against you. People never feel good about buying something if they believe they can get the same thing for less elsewhere. In other words, they want an expensive thing and will spend the money to get it, but only if they feel they're getting a good deal. If they feel they could get a better deal somewhere else, off they go, and you lose the sale.

Your objective, therefore, is to use a high price to heighten attractiveness, yet sell at a lower price to give people a good deal. This is called the *Expensive-Deal Strategy*. When you implement the Expensive-Deal Strategy, you have the most powerful pricing structure possible in effect.

Here are the guidelines for implementing the Expensive-Deal Strategy:

- **For high-ticket items, which the consumer buys irregularly (less than once a year), discount your price.** Automobile dealers, for example, have been using this technique for years. Furniture and major appliance retailers are always having a sale of one kind or another, almost never selling at the suggested retail price. Hotels always charge less than the posted room rates. And few people ever sell a home without coming down from the original asking price.

- **For small-ticket items, which the consumer buys with some regularity (more than once a year), maintain price.** Otherwise, you condition people to haggle over price or to hold off buying until the next inevitable sale comes along. Besides, you want the buyer to feel you already are offering the lowest price possible, and that no additional discount from the already-low price should be expected.

- **Let the consumer "earn" a discount.** You can maintain your price, yet offer a discount at the same time, by allowing the buyer to earn the discount. What do you want your customer to do? Once you identify that, simply offer them a discount for doing it. Here are three types of earned discounts:

  1. Quantity discount. The more they buy, the lower the unit price.

  2. Payment discount. For example: If they pay 100 percent up front, they get a significant discount. (This, incidently, is worth rewarding. Up-front payment really helps your cash flow.)

  3. Package discount. A "package" is two or more items bundled together and sold for one package price. Like Microsoft Office, or the "value meals" at fast food restaurants. The package price is less than what you would pay if you bought each item separately.

     Use your imagination to create great packages. Here are some of the better ones I've seen:

     A hardware store created a gas grill package that included

four items: the grill, assembly of the grill, a full propane tank, and delivery to your home. They sell a ton of these packages every spring!

An optometrist offered a package with three items: a new pair of regular glasses, a new pair of sunglasses, and a $20 trade-in allowance on an old pair of glasses. The trade-in allowance was especially attractive, since it makes the customer feel they are getting something for their old glasses, instead of just throwing them out. They collect cartons full of old glasses (which are donated to some charitable organization) and sell an equal number of new glasses.

Some radio stations have a hard time selling commercials to air in the midnight-to-6 A.M. time period. So they creatively package as follows: Buy x number of commercials (called "spots") in the 6 A.M.-to-midnight time period, and for only 10 percent more money, you'll get an equal number of spots in the midnight-to-6 A.M. time period. Not only does this package fill up commercial "availabilities" in the midnight-to-6 A.M. period, it brings in additional revenue. And the client gets a very good deal.

Automobile manufacturers and dealers are great packagers. They offer rebates, low financing, options packages, trade-in allowances, and so on.

You can get packaging ideas from other business in other industries, then adapt them to your business. Just follow the Expensive-Deal Strategy: Use a high price to help establish high value, then offer packages to give the buyer a good deal.

POWER-ATTRACTOR CHECKLIST

Run each of your ads, commercials, promotions, and contests through this check list. More than likely, you won't be able to use all the power-attractors all the time, but one or two is all you need to make a big difference.

1. Are you building familiarity by constantly exposing your logo as often as possible? If you have a physical location, can patrons see your logo wherever they look?

2. Can you restrict your product's or service's availability some-what? Can you suddenly and surprisingly restrict the time allotted to purchase your item? Is the nature of your product such that making it smaller increases its perceived value?

3. Can you play up the local or distant origin of your product? Can you create customer loyalty by pitting your locally produced item against "foreign" competition? Can you create an aura or mystique by emphasizing the exotic, distant origin of your item?

4. Are you attaching a relatively high price to your product or service, yet offering the buyer ways to buy it for less?

Chapter Seven

Putting People into Decision Making Mode

It's time for a quiz. Relax, it's multiple choice. There are no right or wrong answers. I just want to determine what mood you're in right now.

Question: Based on your present mood, which one of the following activities would you rather do right now, assuming you had to put this book down and engage in one of them?

A. Play a round of golf (or any other sport you like).

B. Call a friend and chit-chat on the phone.

C. Turn on the television and watch a movie.

D. Go to the mall and shop for some new clothes.

If you choose either A or D, you're in *Decision Making Mode,* or *DMM.* Engaging in any sporting activity requires concentration and many instantaneous decisions on your brain's part. Shopping requires perhaps less concentration and not-so-instantaneous decisions, but decisions none the less.

If you chose either B or C, you're out of DMM at the moment. Neither chatting with a friend nor watching a movie requires a string of decisions. Your brain's decision-making function can take a rest when you engage in either of these activities. (Technically, all activity requires the brain to made decisions. But some decisions, like choosing words when you speak with a friend or moving your eyes as you watch a movie, are so subconscious and insignificant we don't count them.)

TO DECIDE OR NOT TO DECIDE

The brain likes to avoid any unnecessary activity as a means of self-preservation. It tries to expend the least amount of energy to accomplish its tasks and will therefore take the easier route whenever possible. Making decisions requires more brain activity than not making decisions. The natural tendency is for the brain to avoid DMM, since DMM is work. Kicking the brain into DMM usually requires some expenditure of energy to begin with, and even more executing the subsequent decisions.

That doesn't mean the brain is always trying to avoid DMM. Sometimes the brain wants to be in DMM. This happens when the resulting feeling, let's say emotional stimulation, is greater and more pleasurable than the work it takes — the decisions one must make — to generate it. That's why you enjoy getting on the golf course or playing a video game and making all those decisions . . . it's fun.

There are times when you feel like making decisions and times when you don't. You're in DMM at times, and out of DMM at times. Your brain shifts between the two modes, directing you to engage in decision-making activity or non-decision-making activity to keep you comfortably balanced.

THE SIGNIFICANCE OF DMM

A person must be in DMM in order to make a purchase decision. That is not exactly the same thing as saying that a person is in DMM each time he makes a purchase. He could, after all, decide to purchase a product on Monday, but not get around to making the purchase until Friday. By the time he actually makes the purchase, he may well be out of DMM. The act of purchasing is not really important. It's the *purchase decision,* which precedes the act, that counts.

Speaking of the time lag between the purchase decision and the actual act of purchasing, isn't that really what a buying habit is? A buying habit is nothing more than an old decision that is repeatedly acted upon sometime after the original buy decision has been made. I'll bet you know someone that shops at the same grocery store week after week, month after month, year after year. At one time that person was in DMM with regard to grocery shopping. She made a decision; she chose a store to patronize. After that, she dropped out of DMM with regard to grocery stores and simply keeps acting upon the old decision over and over.

Buying habits are good for the marketer. They help protect you from having your customers snaked by a competitor. Yes, it works the other way around, too. You must often break a buying habit to gain a new customer. But with all the ammunition you're getting from this book, you'll be breaking buying habits and gaining new customers left and right.

One more point before we move on: Simply because a person is in DMM doesn't necessarily mean he will choose to purchase your product or service. He may choose to purchase your competitor's product or none at all. In DMM, a purchase decision of some kind will be made. The outcome of that decision is not significant at the moment. For now, just be aware that a person must be in DMM in order to decide to buy.

HOW MARKETING AND DMM RELATE

When a person's brain is in DMM with regard to your particular product or service, it is ready and willing to make a purchase decision. But that doesn't occur very often. Most of the time a person is out of DMM with regard to any particular product or service. In other words, out of the 604,800 seconds that comprise a seven-day week, someone might spend eight seconds thinking about buying your product. That's a whole lot of time they're *not* thinking about buying your product. And that's if they think about buying once each week. If the nature of your product or service is such that the typical buyer might consider buying only once a year or so, they are spending around 99.99999 percent of their life without even the slightest thought of buying from you.

So . . . here's a key question: If most people are out of DMM most of the time, what good does it do you to market to them? A marketing message that reaches someone out of DMM is a wasted message, isn't it? They're certainly not going to act upon it if they're not in DMM, right?

Yes, it is true most of your marketing messages will reach people who are out of DMM at the time. But, such an impression is not wasted. When people are out of DMM, their brains are still receiving information. They're susceptible to influence, although they may not be ready to make a buying decision yet.

In the previous chapter, and later in this book, I talk about the importance of penetrating the subconscious mind and making impressions. Most of this happens when the receiver is out of DMM. But the impressions are made nevertheless, and they mount up. *The cumulative effect of numerous impressions received out of DMM can cause the brain to kick into DMM.*

In addition, your accumulated marketing impressions are pre-conditioning the receiver to favor your product or service when his or her brain does shift into DMM. That's really what top-of-mind awareness is all about. Whatever brand you first recall when your brain kicks into DMM is very likely to be the brand that made the most significant impression back when you were out of DMM.

Timing is a factor. Since purchase decisions occur only when people are in DMM, and since (a) DMM regarding a particular product or service occurs rarely, and (b) different people go into DMM at different times, there may be a time lag between your marketing activity and the sales result it produces. In fact, this is usually the case.

Many times marketers will engage in trial-and-error marketing — try something and see if results come in. If there are no results, abandon the marketing plan and try something else. They never give their campaign a chance to germinate. (Remember waste of marketing money number three: marketing turmoil?) Results don't always show up immediately after you begin marketing. Results show up when people are in DMM. And it may take a number of impressions, over a length of time, to get them into DMM.

INSTIGATING DMM IS ONE OF YOUR PRIMARY MARKETING OBJECTIVES

In order for someone to purchase your product or service, he or she must first be in DMM at some point prior to the actual purchase behavior. Therefore, one of your ongoing objectives is to instigate DMM. By instigating DMM, purchases can happen faster and in greater volume.

Think of the purchase of your product or service as a three-step mental process. The first step occurs when an individual's brain goes into DMM ("Perhaps I should buy a new lawn mower."). The second step occurs when the individual chooses a particular brand ("Those Acme mowers seem pretty good."). The third step occurs when he or she makes the actual purchase decision ("I'm going to buy that Acme mower."). The subject of this chapter is step one — getting people into DMM. The rest of this book deals with getting people to choose your brand and executing the purchase.

DMM STIMULI

What causes the brain to go into and out of DMM? Well, dropping out of DMM is the brain's default state. It will automatically go there in the absence of any DMM-activating stimuli. It will also go there immediately following a decision.

There are five types of DMM-activating stimuli that cause the brain to go into DMM. Two are out of the marketer's control. The other three can be brought about or enhanced through good marketing.

What the Marketer Cannot Affect

• **Acute need.** Your television set breaks down, so it's time to buy a new one. Your food supply is running low, so off you go to the grocery store. Your wardrobe needs updating, so you decide it's time to go shopping. Notice of a lawsuit arrives, and suddenly you're in need of an attorney.

In these cases, it's the growing or sudden need to acquire something that activates DMM. The marketer needn't be concerned with this; you cannot control when someone runs out of shampoo (although you can be ready to sell to them when they do).

- **Periodic self-activation.** Rarely does a person make a decision once and continue acting upon it ever afterward. Even without any outside stimuli, a person usually reactivates DMM with regard to a particular product or service periodically.

    This self-activation is not one you can directly affect. But noting its existence tells you that people will consider buying your product or service on occasion anyway, even if you do very little to instigate it.

What the Marketer Can Affect

- **Collected impressions.** As I mentioned earlier, the cumulative weight of a number of persuasive impressions received out of DMM can cause the brain to kick into DMM. Like the drops of water that accumulate in a precariously balanced bucket . . . one more drop and the entire bucket tips over.

    The latest direct mail campaign, the latest billboard campaign, or the latest television, radio, or print campaign may very well be the drop of water that causes the entire bucket to tip. You've kicked many people into DMM at once, and your sales rise. This happens quite often to marketers that maintain a healthy dose of marketing activity on a regular basis. They've got enough people with full buckets out there who only need one more drop to kick into DMM.

    But marketers who do not engage in a healthy amount of marketing activity on a regular basis do not benefit from the effects of collected impressions, because no impressions are collecting in people's minds. Once every few years such marketers execute some ad or promotional campaign and get disappointing results. That's because they're only beginning to fill buckets instead of tipping them over.

Remember when we talked about bursting through the results threshold in Chapter 4? We said that to get results, you must do it big. Now you know why. Ninety percent of the marketing you do fills the bucket — it builds upon itself — and is therefore valuable, but may not be enough to activate DMM in many people. Ten percent of the marketing you do is the final drop that activates DMM and makes all of your expenditures pay off.

Collected impressions are very potent. They produce results, even though the results don't always show up immediately. Some people have empty buckets, and you've got to do a good deal of filling before they'll tip over. Understanding this will prevent you from uprooting or cancelling your marketing activity during certain times when it may appear results are not forthcoming.

- **Emotional stimulation.** Sometimes a buying habit can become too comfortable. It can become dull and boring. When an alternative stimulates the emotions in some way that the habit does not, DMM can be activated. If this weren't true, few married people would stray or get divorced. After all, once two people commit to one another, the brain is supposed to drop out of DMM with regard to mating. But when the brain finds itself lacking the type of emotional stimulation it craves, it will be most receptive to another source that can supply the desired stimulation.

- **A different or better outcome.** People will go into DMM when they perceive that a different and/or better outcome is possible. Something new or different can break a buying habit and snap a person into DMM.

Why are laundry detergent makers always sticking the words "New" and "Improved" on their boxes? They're telling us that the outcome, presumably a cleaner or brighter wash, is different from what it used to be.

Earlier I said the marketer can't control when the consumer runs out of shampoo or when his or her television set breaks down. But by introducing something new, something technologically advanced or of a newer style or design, you can often activate DMM before an acute need would otherwise activate it.

General Motors discovered back in the 1920s that people would buy new cars because they simply wanted the latest model, not because their old car no longer ran. Clothing marketers are constantly coming out with newer, different styles, for the same reason. And in the world of technology, computer hardware and software manufacturers are always improving their products so people will go into DMM often and keep buying the latest.

HOW TO INSTIGATE DMM

Here are the two things you should do on an on-going basis to get people into Decision Making Mode:

- **Step 1: Maintain marketing activity.** When you keep up a steady dose of powerful marketing activity, you empower each individual advertisement, commercial, promotion, piece of publicity, and contest to produce immediate results. Each lays on top of the cumulated weight of the others and each acts as the final drop that fills and tips buckets, thus activating DMM in many people at once.
- **Step 2: Periodically improve or update some aspect(s) of your product or service.** You must improve or alter your product or service from time to time, not only to keep your existing customers from straying to another brand, but to kick others into DMM so they'll consider buying your product or service.

Chapter Eight

The Power of Projection

The last time you purchased a new car, did you test drive it beforehand? And the last time you bought a new suit, dress, or coat, did you try it on first? The last time you bought a piece of furniture, did you imagine what it would look like in your home before you decided to buy it? And the last time you decided to go on vacation, did you imagine what it would be like to be there before you decided to go?

Yes, yes, yes, and yes. But why? Let's take them one at a time. Why did you test drive the car before buying? To determine how it runs and handles, of course. But that was only part of the reason. Actually, you test drove the car mainly to help your brain experience the *feelings* you would get if you owned it. You wanted to experience what it would *feel like* when other people on the road saw you in the car . . . when your neighbors saw it parked in your driveway . . . when your co-workers saw you getting into it and out of it in the parking lot. You imagined what it would feel like to experience these things. Actually climbing into the car and taking it for a spin helped you do so.

When you tried on a suit or dress, you did so to determine how well it fit and whether or not it looked good on you. But another reason you tried it on was to create the feelings you would experience wearing the item to work, to a social function, or wherever (you might even imagine yourself at a specific event wearing the item).

SAMPLE FEELINGS

The brain has an insatiable desire to produce *sample feelings*. That is, it produces certain feelings ahead of time that actually represent the future feelings it would experience if one owned the item in question.

Think about it. When you shop for furniture, don't you imagine how each piece would look in your home? Don't you try to feel what it would be like when others see the furniture in your home? How about vacation sites? Don't you base your choice on the feelings you experience as you imagine what it would be like to actually be there?

ENVISIONING IS THE BRAIN'S FAVORITE SPORT

Your brain attempts to produce sample feelings before each and every decision you make, including each purchase decision. Sample feelings, after all, are a great tool to aid in your decision-making process.

The method your brain uses to produce sample feelings is a process called *envisioning*.

Envisioning something is like watching a movie in which the person doing the envisioning is the lead character (like watching yourself in old home videos). The obvious difference between watching a real movie with your eyes and envisioning one in your mind is that the envisioned movie really doesn't exist. It's just a mental mirage created by the brain to produce sample feelings.

Most of the envisioning your brain does is done at the subconscious level. You don't even know you're doing it most of the time. Like the last time you walked by the fresh fruit aisle and decided to put a bunch of bananas in your cart. The mental vision of you and/ or your family eating and enjoying the bananas happened so fast and so far below your level of consciousness you were totally unaware of it. But it happened nonetheless. If the vision hadn't been created, and a positive sample feeling experienced, your brain wouldn't have instructed you to buy the bananas.

PROJECTION AND ENVISIONING

As a marketer, you want people to envision owning your product or service. You want them to experience sample feelings so pleasurable and strong that they feel compelled to buy.

You foster envisioning of your product or service through the technique called *projection*. Projecting a vision is like showing a mental movie — a movie you produced as you saw fit — a movie that shows your product or service in use by the prospective buyer — a movie that helps the prospect produce positive sample feelings.

Because sample feelings play such a strong role in the purchase decision process, projection is an extremely effective marketing technique. Moreover, projection runs into virtually no resistance by the receiver. A person's mind is wide open for as much projection as you care to supply. That's because people want to envision; they do it all the time. When you project an image, you help them envision it. Working together, not in opposition, the marketer and consumer are on the same side — as is the case with every demand-creating technique I discuss in this book.

When you project an image, you are painting a mental picture for the prospect to see and experience. Through projection, you take a person on a mental trip into the future . . . a future that includes the ownership of your product or service and the resulting feeling.

Projection is most often achieved through advertising. It is created by the ways you word your copy or dialog and how you compose your photos or moving images. This will become clear as we next discuss how to implement projection.

HOW TO USE PROJECTION IN YOUR ADVERTISING

Projection is not a difficult technique to use. Simply follow these two steps:

- **Step 1: Depict one or more people experiencing the feelings one gets through either actual product usage or as a result of product usage.** Here are some examples for randomly selected products and services.

     Boat. Without projection: Show the boat as it appears in the showroom or parked at a dock. Projection: Depict people having the time of their lives, laughing and screaming with excitement in the boat as it moves through the water.

     Perfume. Without projection: Show a woman putting on perfume in front of the mirror. Projection: Show a woman out on the town attracting male attention or in the company of an adoring man.

     Radio station. Without projection: Show pictures of your personalities or news events the station has covered. Projection: Show people listening at work, in the car, and at home. Show people winning your contest while listening.

     Legal services. Without projection: Show the senior partners sitting at their desks talking about their services. Projection: Show a judge declaring "judgment for the plaintiff!" and a client hugging the attorney. Or show the opposing council shaking in the boots when they find out your law firm is representing their opponent.

     House paint. Without projection: Show a homeowner painting his house. Projection: Show a homeowner beaming with pride as he and a neighbor admire his freshly painted house.

     Politician. Without projection: Talk about what a dirty rotten scoundrel your opponent is. Projection: Show happy people who have benefitted from improvements you made once in office.

- **Step 2: Word your copy in after-the-fact fashion, as through the reader already owns your product or service.** Here are some examples:

Without projection: "Come experience the beauty and seren-ity of an Alaskan vacation." Projection: "You are surrounded by beauty and bathed in serenity in Alaska."

Without projection: "Tune in Tuesday night at nine for 'Spin City.' Projection: "You'll see 'Spin City' Tuesday night at nine."

Without projection: "Come see our fine selection of Kenmore washers and dryers, on sale now through Sunday." Projec-tion: "Your new Kenmore washer and dryer are waiting for you now at Sears . . . and they're on sale through Sunday."

THINK PROJECTION

Projection is one of those small things that produces a big result. Most of the time, it costs you no more to utilize projection in your advertising than not utilizing it. A few simple structural adjustments in your wording, dialog, or visuals will do the trick.

PART 3

IGNITING DEMAND

In Part 1, you built your marketing jet. In Part 2, you taxied down the runway. Now you're about to lift off.

Marketers often have difficulty getting demand started, usually because they are unaware of or haven't implemented most of the things we've talked about to this point. Other times it's because they aren't sure what specific actions to take to ignite the spark. Chapters 9 through 12 contain the sparks that ignite demand. When you implement the techniques presented in this part, you'll begin to see the demand needle move.

Chapter Nine

Triggering the Purchase Decision

Is it possible for you to do all the things we've discussed in the first eight chapters, to build a great deal of want and desire, yet still not sell much product? Is it possible for a basketball team to play a great game and still lose? Not only is it possible, but it happens all the time. A marketer makes all the right moves, but the payoff never arrives. "The operation was a success but the patient died" type of thing.

This is something you can avoid very easily once you know how. Then you can be confident your class-A marketing effort will translate into the kind of results you so richly deserve.

LATENT WANT AND ACTIVE WANT

Wanting something doesn't automatically mean you'll buy it, unless you're under 15 years of age. At some age fiscal responsibility begins to take hold (although for some that time never seems to arrive). As one grows into adulthood, one increasingly separates want from the purchase decision. You may want a lot of things, but that doesn't mean you run out today and buy them all.

There are two types of want or desire: *latent want* and *active want*. Latent want occurs when a person decides he wants something (usually a subconscious function) but doesn't go so far as to decide to make the purchase. His mind may say to itself "I want a new Lincoln Continental," but that's as far as it goes. He takes no action.

Active want happens when the person goes one step further and decides to make the purchase. "I want a new Lincoln Continental, and I'm going down to the dealership to buy one!" (This is usually a conscious function.)

To create real demand, the kind that ultimately results in burgeoning sales, you must convert latent want into active want. I call this conversion *triggering the purchase decision.*

Think of a person's mind as a river. Want for your particular product or service which intensifies in her mind is like the water accumulating on one side of a dam. The intensification of want is like the increase of water pressure. The water pressure may be building, but the water still isn't flowing (she hasn't decided to make the purchase). And it won't flow until the dam gates open. This chapter is about opening those gates.

THE LOGIC TRIGGER

The trigger that converts latent want into active want is *logic*. You build the intensity of want and desire primarily through the use of emotion, then you trigger the purchase decision through logic. Like building the water pressure, then opening the gate.

Many people believe the subconscious mind is the logical one and the conscious mind is the emotional once. Actually, it's just the opposite. The subconscious mind determines whether you want something or not; the conscious mind determines whether you take action and buy the item.

A purchase decision, therefore, is primarily a conscious function. And the conscious mind thrives on logic. If it doesn't have one or more strong, logical reasons for purchasing, it may feel too uncomfortable to make the purchase, even though it wants the item.

It behooves you, the marketer, to provide the logic necessary to trigger the purchase decision. Otherwise, a person will find it much easier to forgo purchasing your item than expending the brainpower necessary to concoct their own logical reasons for purchasing.

HOW LOGIC WORKS

What enables logic to trigger a purchase decision? There are three factors:

- **Logic aids communication.** It's immensely easier to explain things in logical terms than in emotional terms. For years there was a running joke among the television production crew of the venerable "American Bandstand" show. They knew that practically every time Dick Clark would ask some teens why they liked a song, they'd say, "It's got a good beat and you can dance to it." It may have been more accurate for a person to say, "The specific integration of vocal and musical sounds in this song induces an emotional reaction in my brain that I find highly pleasurable on the subconscious level, Mr. Clark." But what are the chances of anyone articulating that answer?

  When you purchase something, you want to be able to talk about it. And it's a lot easier to talk about things in logical terms.

- **Logic averts ridicule.** Many of our purchase decisions are potential targets for question or ridicule. When someone questions the wisdom behind your purchase of that new, expensive sports car, which of the following answers sounds flakier and more subject to ridicule, and which sounds more justifiable and sound? "I'm trying to impede my growing feelings of inadequacy by bolstering my perceived sexual attractiveness," or "This baby is maintenance-free and has a great resale value." There's nothing like a strong dose of logical reasoning to squelch a doubter. Remember: Emotion fuels debate, logic settles debate.

- **Logic suppresses guilt.** Sometimes we harbor feelings of guilt that become activated when a purchase is driven strictly by emotion. (Sometimes we even feel "buyer's remorse" a day or two later when the emotion simmers down.) Sometimes an emotion-driven purchase produces contradictory feelings, as one force — emotional pleasure — and another force — guiltful pain — are activated simultaneously. The two feelings struggle against each other, producing stress and anxiety. The brain searches for a way to end this internal conflict, or better yet, to avoid it in the first place. Thus the purchase is not made.

Logic suppresses feelings of guilt. When enough logic exists (and it may not take much), guilt is averted, and the purchase decision can be made without any resulting stress and anxiety.

EMOTION-LOGIC CONFLICT

Each of us experiences an inherent and recurring conflict between our emotional and logical minds. It's called *emotion-logic conflict*. Left unabated, emotion-logic conflict will produce feelings of discomfort, tension, stress or anxiety. Which in turn has a paralyzing effect, inhibiting a person from making a purchase decision.

Let's take a closer look at emotion-logic conflict and see how we can counteract its effects. Have you or anyone you know ever expressed conflicts like these?

"I really want this new audio-video system (emotion), but my wife would kill me if I bought it (logic)."

"I know I should save my money (logic), but you only live once (emotion)!"

"This outfit is me (emotion)! But if I wait for a sale at the end of the season, I'll save a bundle on it (logic)."

The above examples show how emotion-logic conflict can exist in the mind of any one person. In addition, emotion-logic conflict can exist between two people, as the following examples show.

PERSON ONE: "This house is great! Let's make an offer (emotion)."

PERSON TWO: "I really think we should look at more houses before we jump (logic)."

PERSON ONE: "Wouldn't this hot sports car be great (emotion)?"
PERSON TWO: "There's no trunk space, and not enough protection if you're in an accident (logic)."

PERSON ONE: "Let's go to Maui (emotion)!"
PERSON TWO: "We'd have to go over the budget and see if we can afford it (logic)."

These are all outward expressions of emotion-logic conflicts, which makes it readily apparent to the individuals that the conflicts exist. But most of the time, we are unaware of the emotion-logic conflict going on inside our brain, because most of it happens at the subconscious level. However, we can be aware of the resulting feelings of tension, anxiety, and stress.

Both the emotional and logical minds want to have influence over your behavior, including your purchase decisions. When they conflict, as we just discussed, it can be very difficult for someone to make a purchase. But when the marketer supplies both emotion-based persuasion and logic-based persuasion, the emotional mind and the logical mind both get some gratification. As the two minds become satisfied, they stop conflicting. Then the subsequent purchase sails through without opposition, much like a bill moving through Congress when both the House and Senate agree.

HOW TO USE LOGIC TO TRIGGER THE PURCHASE DECISION

Every advertisement and commercial you produce should contain some emotion-based persuasion and some logic-based persuasion. You know why. Emotion produces want and desire, and logic triggers the purchase decision. Here are the procedures:

- **Step 1: Use a 9:1 emotion-logic ratio.** Or another way of looking at it: 90 percent of each ad or commercial should be devoted to emotion-intensive information, 10 percent to logic-intensive information. Why such an imbalance between the two? It takes a good deal of effort to build want and desire, but only a small amount of logic to trigger the purchase decision. Think of that dam we talked about earlier. The water builds up over time, increasing the pressure against the wall. All it takes is one small opening in the gate for the water to come gushing forth.

Here's an example. Pontiac's "Driving Excitement" campaign mentioned earlier uses both emotion and logic, in the 9:1 ratio. In the television version, the car moves down water-slicked roadway in an exotic location at night, while youthful members of both sexes interact. Tilted camera angles, fast edits, and energetic music all contribute to the electric mood. This is the emotional part. Then at the very end, the factory financing or rebate information appears on the screen, with an announcer telling you what a great deal you can get. This is the logical part. The emotion produces the desire, and the logic provides the reasoning one needs to act upon the desire. (In fact, Pontiac sometimes uses the tag line "Excitement. Well Built." That's emotion followed by logic in a three-word slogan.)

- **Step 2: Present emotion first, logic second.** The sequence is important. You build want and desire first, then you trigger the purchase decision.
- **Step 3: Use wording that is easy to repeat.** You want to spoon-feed logic to the receivers in a manner that makes it easy for them to spit it back . . . word for word.

Radio stations do this all the time. A line like "We play the kind of music everyone at work can agree on" enables a person to use that very line to rebut someone who questions his or her choice of radio station.

I do it also. Some of my sales material contains the line "Rick Ott is relevant, intriguing, and entertaining." I've now given the reader the ammunition they need to justifying hiring me to speak at their next convention or meeting. When someone says to them "Who are we bringing in to keynote our conference?," they can reply "Rick Ott. He's relevant, intriguing, and entertaining." Neat how that works.

- **Step 4: Keep your logic statements short and quick.** To foster verbalization, you need one or two short, clear, logical sentences. Avoid cute or overly-clever wording that might confuse.
- **Step 5: Justify the emotion.** Hopefully your commercial, ad, web site, or brochure is successful in arousing the receiver's emotions. Remember, however, that some degree of emotion-logic conflict may also be created. Therefore, your logic statement(s) must negate the conflict to make your message really effective.

  You should provide a logical reason why the emotion (whichever emotion you're stimulating) is justified. For example, say you design the emotion-intensive part of your ad to arouse the joy or excitement emotion. You also know that the receiver's logical mind may be opposing the emotion, producing guilt or some other counter-joyous emotion. (If you've ever witnessed people having a lousy time while on an exotic vacation, you're seeing the result of emotion-logic conflict.) So one of your logic statements could be "You work hard and deserve some rest and relaxation," or "Hard work deserves reward." The idea is to give the logical mind some reasoning it will agree with, thus averting its tendency to conflict with the emotional mind.

  Your emotion-justifying line(s) may simply be one or two sentences contained in the body of your copy, or it could be contained in your slogan. McDonald's old "You deserve a break today" campaign is one example. L'Oreal tells you "You're worth it," which justifies spending the money on an pricy product. Miller Beer shows people working hard, sweating, accomplishing . . . then says "Now it's Miller time." In Miller's case, they know people can sometimes have a hard time justifying drinking beer. By showing people working then drinking, they're sending the message that it's okay to drink the beer because you've "earned" it through a hard day's work. The logical mind agrees, and off people go to purchase Miller.

Chapter Ten

Pre-Process for Instant Impact

As one of my clients recently observed, "It's not easy making an impact. We can say whatever we want, and it either goes in one ear and out the other . . . or it never even goes in one ear at all!" Such are the woes of our over-communicated society.

How do you make a significant impact on people when they're bombarded by a never-ending stream of marketing messages each day, and are "selectively perceiving" only a small percentage of them? The answer to that question is the subject of this chapter. You are about to learn of a simple psychological technique that has the power to get your message past a person's perception filters and make a strong impact — instantly.

And that's not all. In addition to making an instant, strong impact, you'll be able to arrange things so that your brand name is recalled instantly whenever a person first thinks of whatever type of product or service you market. You no longer have to spend decades working to achieve top-of-mind awareness. Now, you can obtain stellar results in a relatively short time.

THE BRAIN'S INFORMATION PROCESSING SYSTEM

To learn how to achieve both instant impact and instant, top-of-mind recall, you must first understand how the brain handles information.

As each of the five senses — sight, hearing, touch, taste, and smell — receives information (which happens constantly), it instantaneously sends the information to the brain. The brain must determine what to do with that information, by making a never-ending series of decisions about what is important, what is not important, what needs to be acted upon, what doesn't need to be acted upon, and so forth. As a result of these decisions, your information — your brand name or logo, for example — either makes an impression or it doesn't. Unfortunately for most marketers, their name or logo makes no impact at all, or a weak impact at best, most of the time. For you, that is about to change.

How Processing Works

Say a person sees your logo in a print ad. That piece of information, your logo, travels through nerves from the eyes to the brain. When it arrives, the brain tries to determine what your logo *means,* or how *relevant* it is. The search for meaning and relevancy is called *processing.*

To process your logo or brand name, the brain begins performing a specific one- or two-step maneuver to determine just what it means and how relevant it is. Once this determination is made, processing stops.

Let's walk through the steps so you can see exactly how processing is accomplished.

1. You see the word "Brensello's" on a sign along the highway. (I made this word up for purposes of this illustration. Any similarity with an actual person, place, company, or product is coincidental and should be ignored.) In its quest for meaning and relevancy, your brain begins processing the word "Brensello's" by executing step one: searching its memory for information that matches. In other words, it looks for some degree of familiarity. If this latest piece of information — the most recent sighting of the word "Brensello's" —

matches up with any stored information in your memory, your brain will assign the same meaning to the new information as the stored meaning from its memory bank. For example, you recall having eaten at Brensello's; your memory indicates it's a submarine sandwich shop. Therefore, the latest sighting of the word "Brensello's" has been assigned a meaning, and processing stops.

Everything that has happened so far, from seeing the word "Brensello's," to searching your memory, discovering a match, and assigning a meaning, took place at the subconscious level, and in a split second. Consciously, you may not have even been aware of the Brensello's sign, but subconsciously you saw it and processed it faster than a computer.

2. But let's say the new information does not match up with anything in your memory. Your brain then continues to process by executing step two, which is a decision to take one of two alternative routes.

- **Route A:** It seeks additional information. It tries to answer the question, What is "Brensello's"? A brand of ice cream? A shoe store? The name of a street? A magazine? What?

  If your brain decides to take this route, it must actively go on an information-gathering expedition. It must now kick the word "Brensello's" up to the conscious level of attention and deal with it there. Once this happens, everything slows down considerably. Instant impact can be made only subconsciously. Once the brain decides to deal with information at the conscious level, impact can be made but it happens much slower.

  At any rate, your brain now directs you to take specific information-gathering behavior, such as to ask the person riding in the car with you what "Brensello's" is, or to look intently at the building on which the "Brensello's" sign is attached to see what it looks like. Or it directs you to any other type of activity that would possibly give it the information it needs to assign the word "Brensello's" a meaning. Since this route requires conscious attention and effort, it happens a whole lot less than you might think. Instead, the brain will take the easy way, Route B.

  (Route A actually involves two other functions, *categorization* and *evaluation*. Your brain must categorize information as a means of organizing it all. Evaluation involves determining whether the information is good or bad for you. I won't go into greater detail about categorization or evaluation, since a deeper understanding of all this stuff is not necessary, and I am trying to keep it simple.)

- **Route B:** Your brain rejects the information. It cannot produce a match between the newly-sighted word "Brensello's" and anything in storage, and it doesn't feel like bothering the conscious mind (which might be thinking of something completely different at the time) with the trivial task of finding meaning. So it determines the word "Brensello's" is irrelevant, and is therefore thrown out. Rejected. Turned away at the gate. This sighting of the word "Brensello's" has made no impact.

Most of the time, the brain will opt for Route B, since it's the route of least resistance. Remember, the brain likes to avoid expending energy. That's why many marketing messages never make much of an impact.

HOW INSTANT IMPACT HAPPENS

Are you still with me? This discussion may seem quite microscopic and detailed, but sharp marketers who aspire to rise above the others will need to know this material. Hang with me and you'll be well rewarded.

What do you want a person's brain to do when it sees your logo or hears your company name? Certainly you don't want the brain to reject it.

Nor do you want the brain to have to make a conscious effort to seek meaning and relevance, since doing so has many disadvantages. For one, it takes longer. And the longer it takes, the weaker the impact. Second, the brain may assign an inaccurate meaning to your product name or logo . . . one that carries a negative connotation. This happens all the time, when additional information about you comes from one of your competitors. When the brain resorts to conscious processing, it does so at the marketer's risk.

The best alternative we've seen yet occurs when the brain successfully matches a piece of newly-received information with previously-received information in memory. When this happens, the new information is assigned a meaning, is determined to be relevant, and is immediately routed to that part of the brain that accepts impressions. Therefore, *when your name or logo matches something in a person's memory, it has made a strong, subconscious impression, in an instant's time.*

So how do you, the marketer, cause this to happen? How do you make sure your logo matches up with the "correct" meaning in people's brains? Must a person be familiar with your logo or name before this can happen? If so, a brand new product or company is handicapped by its unfamiliar name. And what if your product, service, or company has been around for a while, yet most of your logo sightings have been rejected by people's brains? You could spend a ton of money on additional logo exposures, but those too might be rejected because they still don't match with anything in memory.

How would you feel if you knew that each and every time people saw your logo or heard your name, a processing match occurred in their brains, and your logo or name made an instant, strong impression? Would that improve your overall impact by a significant degree? You'd better believe it would! It wouldn't take long for demand to rise and sales results to show!

MAKE INSTANT IMPACT BY PRE-PROCESSING

The secret lies in a technique called *pre-processing.* When you preprocess, you avert the brain's processing function altogether by providing the brain with a relevant meaning to go along with your name or logo. In other words, the brain receives your logo and a meaning at the same time, thus negating its need to search for a meaning. Pre-processing results in an even stronger and quicker impression than when the brain processes and matches. And it happens every time the brain receives your brand name, company name, or logo!

You pre-process by providing the brain with a piece of information — a special word — that it is already familiar with, and which carries a positive or desirable connotation. We call this special word a *pre-processed word.* You simply attach your pre-processed word to your name or logo.

When you pre-process, you are doing for the mind what Gatorade does for the body. The body converts sugar into glucose, which it then uses for energy. Gatorade contains glucose, which is pre-processed sugar. When the body receives Gatorade, it does not need to go through the process of converting sugar into glucose, for glucose has already been received. Instant energy results.

Pre-Processing Examples

The oldest and best example of pre-processing actually dates back to the early 1900s. For many years, Coca-Cola had the word "Drink" attached to their logo. In fact, it was practically part of the logo. Wherever the Coca-Cola logo appeared, the word "Drink" appeared with it (positioned above). "Drink" is a great pre-processed word, for many reasons. One of the first things we all do when we're born is drink. In fact, we all have to drink everyday to live. So everyone is familiar with the word "Drink," and it carries a positive connotation. It can also be used as a verb or a noun, as in "Hold the bottle up to your mouth and drink Coca-Cola (drink used as a verb), and "Drink: Coca-Cola," meaning Coca-Cola is a drink (noun version).*

Another example goes back a few decades. Remember driving through the country and seeing a diner that had the word "EAT" in huge letters above their names? "Eat" is another great pre-processed word. Everyone knows what it means and everyone can relate to it at least three times a day.

I've always advised my radio station clients to put the word "Radio" or "Listen" in front of their logos. Likewise, I advise my television clients to put either "Television" or "Watch" in front of the logos. Remember, the brain needs to know what your logo means, or it'll start processing. It may not know what "K-93" is without the word "Radio" attached. And people spend so much time in front of computer screens they may not realize or remember when they're watching a television station or cable channel.

---

*Coca-Cola used the pre-processed word "Drink" for many years. Around the mid 1970s they changed it to "Enjoy." In the early 1990s, they dropped "Enjoy" and began putting various innocuous words in the pre-processed position. They simply lost sight of its importance over the years. How could Coke engineer a quick and lasting serge in sales at no cost? Go back to the great pre-processed word "Drink" and put it right above the logo where it used to be.

FIGURE 1
Examples of pre-processed logos (fictitious brands).

Look at Figure 1. It contains a few examples of logos (for fictitious products) with pre-processed words attached. Notice the pre-
processed word is always positioned above or to the left of the logo.
Notice also that the pre-processed word can be so ingrained it actu-

ally becomes part of the logo.

THE KEY TO PRE-PROCESSING'S EFFECTIVENESS

I know what you're thinking. "A pre-processed word may help a new product or service gain familiarity, but everyone already knows what my product is," you point out.

There are two problems with that reasoning. First, despite how it may seem, few people know your brand name, and fewer still know what it means. The vast majority of the population — even the majority of your target market — either have never heard of you or have an erroneous impression of you. Very few people in the United States can name the vice president (whomever occupies that position), despite the fact that he or she gets significant, nationwide media exposure. And the executives of that radio station calling itself "K-93" had to be scraped off the floor when they found out many people thought "K-93" was either a bug spray, a household lubricant, or a dog.

Second, telling people what your name or logo means is only part of what you accomplish through pre-processing. At the beginning of this chapter I talked about gaining top-of-mind awareness in a relatively short period of time. This is a by-product of pre-processing that is as important as making an instant impression. Herein lies the real key to the effectiveness of pre-processing. By providing a pre-processed word and attaching it to your name or logo, *you are programming the receiver's brain to store the two — the pre-processed word and logo — together as one piece of information.* When that occurs, your name automatically pops into a person's consciousness when the pre-processed word first flashes in their mind.

Here's how it works: A person gets thirsty. Her brain signals that it wants to drink. This can happen subconsciously or consciously. The latter often happening in the company of another person when one verbally expresses the desire to the other ("Let's get something to drink," or "What would you like to drink?"). The word "Drink" is the trigger word that causes the attached product to shoot up into consciousness. That's why even the world's most recognizable logo, Coca-Cola, would still benefit by using the pre-processed word

"Drink."

By pre-processing, you not only assure your brand name or logo makes an instant, positive impression every time, but you're programming many brains out there to recall your name instantly when prompted. The results can be dramatic and fast! No wonder pre-processing is such a powerful and important technique to adopt.

HOW TO PRE-PROCESS

- **Step 1: Choose a pre-processed word.** The ideal pre-processed word is descriptive, has a positive connotation, and is likely to come to mind often. A noun is best, a verb second best (a word that can be both a noun and verb is even better).

  For example, the pre-processed word "Restaurant" indicates what you are, which is good. The word "Eat" is less descriptive, but it is more likely to come up in conversation, so it works well (tackiness aside). The word "Hungry" would work well also because it indicates you are a source of food, and it is likely to come to mind often.

- **Step 2: Link your pre-processed word to your brand name or logo (in auditory or visual form).** It's better to position your pre-processed word before your name or logo. Remember, your pre-processed word comes to mind first, and your name rides on its coattails, such as when your friend gets you into the event by telling the doorkeeper, "He's with me."

  Look at Figure 1, on page 113, once again. The pre-processed word "Fun!" is positioned above and to the left of the name "Brad's." After a number of impressions are made on a person's subconscious, what will pop into that person's mind when she thinks of having some fun? More than likely, the name "Brad's."

  This can also be done verbally. In a radio or television commercial, the voice can say "When you're hungry, Brensello's is the place to go." Notice that the words "hungry" and "Brensello's" are right next to each other, in the proper order.

  Once you link your pre-processed word and logo, keep it that way. It's a marriage that shouldn't come apart easily. In fact, your pre-processed word can become part of your logo. The two become one, which is what you're trying to make happen in the receiver's brain anyway.

EXTREME PRE-PROCESSING

The ultimate in pre-processing occurs when your brand name and pre-processed word are one and the same. How is this achieved?

Consider these examples: Tire America, Computer City, Comfort Inn, Food Lion, Pizza Hut, Motel 6, Subway, and Casino Windsor. What makes the aforementioned brand names different than Wonder Bread, Minute Rice, Fast Frame, Jiffy Lube, and Betty's Delicatessen? In the former list, the pre-processed word comes first. The latter list contains brand names in which the pre-processed word comes second. Although all these brand names are fine, the ones in which the pre-processed word comes first make better use of the pre-processing concept, and are therefore stronger.

TWO TRAPS TO AVOID

There are two traps that you must avoid before pre-processing will work it's magic for you.

First, do not let the seeming awkwardness of pre-processing bother you. Having a pre-processed word attached to the front end of your brand name may seem strange, out of place, or illogical. That's okay! Remember, people are not consciously scrutinizing and analyzing your logo as you are. Besides, you'll get used to it in time; then it won't seem awkward to you at all.

Second, you must keep in mind that pre-processing really happens in the subconscious mind of the receiver. The impressions you make through pre-processing are all received subconsciously, and the recall of your name happens subconsciously. A person doesn't know why the name Brad's suddenly comes to mind when he thinks of doing something that's fun, he's just aware that it does. (Sometimes, the awareness isn't even there. He just goes to Brad's and makes a purchase without ever realizing how or why he thought of Brad's.)

Conscious vs. Subconscious Impressions

Many marketers overrate the value of making conscious impressions and underrate the value of making subconscious impressions. That's why you see so many nebulous "teaser" ad campaigns. They want to "arouse curiosity" and "create talk" by getting people to wonder what the ad is all about. This is the exact opposite of pre-processing. It not only requires the brain to process, it also makes it *difficult* for the brain to find a meaning. How many times do you think such an ad is rejected by the brain? My estimate is 999 times out of 1,000 sightings result in rejection, with no impact and no result.

On the other hand, if you pre-process your ads — even to the point where you showed little more than your pre-processed word and logo — how many instant subconscious impressions will you make? How about 1,000 impressions out of 1,000 sightings?! Of course, you may not "create talk" with such an ad, but so what? If no one is talking about your advertising, there's a good chance it's working well, albeit subconsciously.

Let me repeat a point I made earlier. Conscious impressions are fine, they can work. But if you care only about making impressions on the conscious level, you are forfeiting a huge amount of effectiveness. Pre-processing makes impressions on the subconscious level, and thus affects the vast amount of human behavior that the subconscious mind controls. Besides, subconscious impressions are easier to make, and much more efficient.

Chapter Eleven

Attract New Customers by Widening Your Appeal

One of the greatest ways to start and build demand is to widen the appeal range of your product or service. Doing so can result in a rather dramatic leap in demand within a short period of time. Unfortunately, for every one marketer than understands how to go about widening appeal properly, nine other marketers either misunderstand the process and botch it up, or don't even believe in widening appeal at all and thus never attempt it. Nine out of ten marketers, therefore, suffer from self-inflicted demand limitations. If you want to be the one out of ten that rises above, you'll enjoy this chapter.

Widening the appeal of a product or service is really a function of targeting. Since even the simplest discussion of targeting can get confusing, we're going to look at the targeting process in a way that makes it easy to understand and discuss. This way of looking at things may be quite different from what you're used to, and may use terminology in different ways from what you're used to, so let's start by establishing a common understanding.

THE CORE AND FRINGE

For almost every type of product or service in existence, there exists a number of consumers who are heavy users of same. Heavy users buy and use the type of product or service often. They are collectively referred to as *core* buyers or consumers, and are defined mainly using standard demographic measures (the psychographic dimension will be addressed in Chapters 15 and 16). For example, core beer drinkers are males between 18 and 44 years of age. Core buyers of tennis shoes are males and females between the ages of 16 and 28 who reside in middle income or higher households and who play tennis often.

The core is almost always a thin segment of the overall population, a small slice of the pie. When your marketing is designed to reach and affect only the core, as when a tennis shoe marketer crafts ads and buys media to hit middle income-plus people between the ages of 16 and 28 who play tennis, you're said to be "targeting your core."

People who buy and use a product or service in smaller quantity or less frequently than the core are called *fringe* consumers. Demographically speaking, the fringe falls outside of your tightly defined core. For the tennis shoe marketer, the fringe may be people under 16 and over 28 who play tennis irregularly or not at all. When you design your marketing to appeal to people outside of your core, you're said to be "targeting your fringe." When you design your marketing to appeal to your fringe as well as your core, you're said to be "targeting your core and fringe."

Core and fringe consumers together compose 100 percent of the potential buying population for your type of product or service. If a person has never or is unlikely ever to buy your type of product, that person falls out of your buying population and is contained in neither the core nor fringe category for your product type.

CORE TARGETING IS NOT THE NAME OF THE GAME

Hardly a week goes by without some marketing or advertising executive reiterating the popular belief that "pinpointing" consumers and "zeroing in" with thinly targeted marketing is the name of the game. Some marketers consider themselves all the wiser as they devise an ever-increasing number of ways to avoid mass marketing and "niche market" only to a thin slice of the consumer pie.

Simple logic would seem to agree. After all, if you're a marketer of athletic shoes, you ought to market to athletes. That's how the athletic shoe industry began . . . shoes made for and marketed to athletes. But some of the major brands of the 1950s, '60s, and '70s, such as Converse, U.S. Keds, P.F. Flyer, and Adidas, never looked beyond the sports-oriented, heavy user core. Then along came Nike and Reebok in the '80s and '90s. They didn't follow simple logic. Instead, they targeted the fringe as well as the core; they designed their marketing to reach and appeal to the light user, the non-athlete. The result? A sales explosion, leaving those core-only brands in the dust. The next time you see someone wearing an athletic shoe while engaging in some non-athletic activity, such as shopping, working around the house, or just lounging around, the chances are he or she will be wearing either Nike or Reebok as opposed to any other brand.

I always get a chuckle when I hear someone trumpeting the advantages of the ever-increasing media fragmentation, as though greater fragmentation (when each media outlet delivers a thinner slice of the pie), is good for the marketer. The media are becoming increasingly fragmented because there are an ever-increasing number of media outlets in existence, forcing each one to end up with a thinner slice of the audience pie. Media fragmentation did not come about because the media decided to do the marketer a favor. If anything, fragmentation makes things more difficult for the marketer, as she must now buy many more media outlets to reach the same number of consumers she previously reached with far fewer outlets.

Of course, the marketer can "take advantage" of the fragmentation and buy fewer media outlets, selecting only those that deliver one's core consumer. Such niche marketing can be advantageous at times, such as when you're launching a new business or new product. As long as you are satisfied with limited sales, and not concerned with sales growth beyond your core, niche marketing may be all you need. But if you're interested in growing your sales revenue, read on.

The Disadvantages of Niche Marketing

When you target your marketing to reach and affect only your core, you're likely to experience three hefty problems.

First, there's a strong chance you're limiting your sales significantly. The video tape recorder was invented by Ampex Corporation. They marketed it to television stations, and made a modest profit over the years. It took the Japanese — masters of mass marketing — to turn the VCR into a mass-market product, and they made tons of money. A lot more potential sales exist beyond your thinly defined core than may be obvious. Besides, you're trying to create demand in a major way, right? If you limit yourself to core-targeted marketing only, you lessen your chances of achieving that objective.

Second, you forfeit the opportunity to enlarge your core. Core enlargement is accomplished by converting light users into heavy users. The only way to do that is to direct some of your marketing toward your fringe and persuade them accordingly.

Third, core-targeted marketing can quickly result in wasted media expenditures. Most marketers think it's the other way around, that targeting beyond their core results in greater waste. Not necessarily so. In truth, the waste of media expenditures can become more severe when you target thinly and niche market than when you spread out and target wider. I'll explain how that happens shortly.

The Core Obsession Trap

A funny thing tends to happen to niche marketers. They come to believe the key to their continued success is to concentrate all their marketing efforts on their core. They end up "super serving" their core, to the extent they totally neglect their fringe. They fall into the *Core Obsession Trap*.

Believe it or not, some marketers are even obsessed with the core of the core! They target so thinly they need a microscope to see what they're doing. A radio station program director once mentioned that their core was a 24-year-old single female who works during the day and goes dancing at night. Sometimes talking about your core in such definitive terms can be useful, as long as you realize that this core-of-the-core bull's-eye represents a relatively small number of people. And that you're going to have to market well beyond this little bull's-eye to move the sales needle.

What makes a marketer fall into the Core Obsession Trap? Here are the three main causes:

First of all, marketers can end up disproportionately serving their core because it's so easy to identify core desires. Your core — the people who are heavy users of your type of product or service — will contain the most vocal consumers. They'll have strong opinions regarding the product or service in question, and they'll readily make their opinions known to you. Conversely, your fringe — light or non-users of your type of product or service — may not have strong opinions, and may not be inclined to say anything at all. So, marketers end up super-serving the vocal minority and ignoring the silent majority.

Second, marketers sometimes willfully design their marketing to super-serve their core because they misunderstand the old "80/20 Rule." The 80/20 Rule isn't really a rule at all, but simply the observation that around 80 percent of your sale revenue will come from around 20 percent of your customers. While it may be useful to consider the 80/20 Rule when directing your sales effort (you wouldn't, for example, want your salespeople concentrating their efforts on the 20 percent that produce the least revenue), it is dangerous to consider it when directing your marketing effort. One of the primary objectives of marketing is to recruit new buyers and get them into that big-spender category. How are you going to do that if you only recognize the people who are already spending heavily? Your marketing must be future focused — designed to reach and find new buyers — if you want your future revenues to be greater than they are now.

The third reason marketers fall into the Core Obsession Trap is what I mentioned earlier. You'll recall I said that it appears core-targeted marketing results in an efficient use of your media dollars, when in fact, the opposite actually occurs. Let's see how that happens.

The Core Maximization Level

The natural forces of the marketplace, which always rule, dictate that you're going to get only so much market share from your core no matter what you do or how long you do it. Once you reach this point, called the *Core Maximization Level*, the marketing money you allocate to increase core buying becomes terribly inefficient.

This is a fact of reality many marketers refuse to acknowledge. They fail to realize there is a practical limit to the amount of core market share they can prudently attain. They fail to understand it can cost a great deal more to boost sales from their core that it can cost to generate an equal increase in sales from their fringe. Consequently, they end up spending thousands upon thousands, or millions upon millions, of dollars trying to suck every quarter point of market share out of their core. Like wretchedly squeezing every last drop of juice out of a spent grapefruit. If a core-obsessed marketer actually calculated how much it cost to gain every fractional point of market share beyond the Core Maximization Level, he'd require electroshock treatment to live another day.

People can only wear so many coats, drink so much cola, make so many copies on the copy machine, or own so many vehicles, regardless of the amount of advertising that reaches them. In other words, your core may be maxed out. Welcome to reality.

Did you ever spend a good chunk of your marketing budget only to realize no appreciable increase in sales? Could it be you were targeting a depleted core? When you reach your Core Maximization Level, you must look to your fringe for revenue growth. Remember, the fringe may be just as likely to purchase your product or service as the core if they have some motivation. You may be surprised how relatively easy it is to increase overall market share when you stop concentrating exclusively on your core and pay a little attention to your fringe.

FRINGE TARGETING IS INEVITABLE

I've got even more news for you. You're going to end up targeting your fringe anyway, whether you like the idea or not. Why? Because of almighty growth. As you know, growth is the master we all serve in the business world. If your revenues aren't growing year after year (or quarter after quarter if you're a public company), you're a dead company. Then all kinds of bad things happen.

So how do you grow your revenues once you've reached the Core Maximization Level? You target the fringe, of course.

Look at what's happening in the financial services industry. Banks are targeting well beyond their core by offering investment brokerage services as well as standard banking services. And traditional investment houses are offering money market accounts with check-writing privileges. So we have banks acting like brokerages and brokerages acting like banks. Why? They've reached their respective Core Maximization Levels, and they've got to attract fringe consumers in order to keep growing.

Fast food marketers are expanding their menus like crazy, trying to attract new consumers. Marketers of sound equipment are now targeting females, who are out of their dominantly male core. Suntan lotions are targeting males, who are outside of their dominantly female core. Office Max and Staples have added printing/copying services to their traditional office supply business. Tuffy Muffler and Midas Muffler dropped the word "Muffler" from their names and became "Auto Service Centers," offering a whole lot more than mufflers.

Politicians know that if they fail to target beyond their core group of supporters, they'll never win an election. It's the fringe voters, the people that don't have strong feelings one way or the other, that politicians must win to put them over the top on election day.

Why do you think so many top marketers buy television time during the Super Bowl every year, at astronomical prices? The Super Bowl draws such a wide and diverse audience they can reach a whole lot of fringe (as well as core) consumers with just one commercial.

Are you happy with your revenue growth? Have you been spending a good amount of marketing money lately and realizing a negligible uptick in sales? You have a choice. Either be satisfied with slow or no growth (not an altogether unwise choice, as long as you have the luxury of no shareholders or lenders leaning on you), or begin targeting your fringe for increased growth.

THE OPTIMUM STRATEGY

Serve both your core and fringe, but neither to such an extreme you ignore the other. It's as simple as that.

There is an exception. As I mentioned earlier, when you first launch a new product, service, or company, you may be wise to be highly niched. Like piercing the skin with a thin, sharp needle, you can penetrate a new market easier than if you advance with a wide, blunt approach. Once you gain entry and have some initial success, however, you may do well by widening your target to include some fringe.

For example, Domino's Pizza spent their first few years targeting their heavy-user core exclusively. This happened to be college students who lived in dormitories.* But once they reached the Core Maximization Level — once these college kids were gobbling as much pizza as they were ever going to — Domino's began targeting their fringe and marketing to people other than college students.

CORE AND FRINGE TENDENCIES

The first step in learning how to work both your core and fringe is to take notice of some key tendencies.
  • **The size of your core and fringe depends on your product.** By definition, your core will have tight demographic parameters.

---

*I happened to be one of them when I attended Michigan State in the early '70s. I recall looking out the window of 12-story Hubbard Hall (which offers a panoramic view of the entire campus) one night and seeing a cadre of Domino's delivery cars (with lighted signs atop) buzzing all over the campus. "What a great I idea," I said to myself, not realizing at the time (a) what a *really* great idea it was, nor (b) how big it would become through superior execution of the idea.

Your fringe, by definition, has much wider demographic parameters. But neither definition says anything about the actual size of each. That would depend on the nature of your product or service.

If you're marketing $1,200 audio turntables, for instance, your core is going to be audiophiles that still believe in vinyl. Demographically, they will be upper-income males between 35 and 55. And your core will be virtually 100 percent of your total consumers, since your fringe will be practically nonexistent. (As the years go on, there are ever fewer people who even remember vinyl records.)

If you're a therapist marketing relationship guidance, your core may be small. This would be females between the ages of 18 and 45 who are experiencing problems in their relationships at the time.* Your fringe, however, may be vast, since everyone wants to have good relationships in the lives, and many people might be inclined to seek help in some form if prompted by good marketing.

- **A person is a core or fringe consumer depending on the item.** There is no such thing as a "core person" or a "fringe person" all the time. A person may be either, and may well switch categories, depending on the product or service in question. For example, Jane may be a core consumer of swimming gear, and a fringe consumer of Italian food. Jack may be a core consumer of computer equipment and a fringe consumer of business suits.
- **Fringe consumers are just as susceptible to influence as core consumers.** Your fringe consumers may have a lower level of interest in your product or service than your core consumers and may buy less frequently, but they do buy and are affected by good marketing. In fact, fringe consumers are often more susceptible to your marketing than core consumers, since core consumers will often formulate opinions based on other, non-advertised information they dig up.

---

*Not that males don't have just as many relationship problems. But females are usually the first to recognize trouble, and are more amenable to outside assistance.

- **Core and fringe consumers have different needs and desires and respond to different marketing stimuli.** In many cases, core consumers of a particular product or service display a high degree of interest in, and enthusiasm for, the product or service. They're "into it." They salivate over detailed information. They're curious about how it's made and the people that produce it. They like to talk about it. They'll join user clubs or in some way participate in never-ending rhetorical discussions with other "enthusiasts."

  The fringe, on the other hand, wants bottom-line information and wants it quickly. The fringe needs to know simply that your product exists, what it does, and what benefits they'll derive from it. The fringe thrives on convenience. The quicker and easier it is and the less thought necessary to begin feeling the benefits, the more they'll buy. A fringe consumer doesn't spend much time thinking about it or talking about it; he or she just buys and moves on.

HOW TO ATTRACT NEW CUSTOMERS BY WIDENING YOUR APPEAL

Widening appeal is nothing more than marketing beyond your core. Here's how to go about it:

- **Step 1: Identify the needs and wants of your core.** To find out whether your core prefers green over blue, or wide over thin, or fast versus slow, or this versus that, simply observe them. Stay close to your core customer and it'll be real obvious what they prefer. Remember, the core likes to talk about the product or service. It doesn't take much prompting to get them to tell you all you need to know to keep them happy.
- **Step 2: Identify the needs and wants of your fringe.** This can be more difficult. The fringe, you'll recall, has a lower level of interest and won't spend the time or energy talking about it. This is one reason marketing research fails so often. A randomly selected sample of users can turn out to include a disproportionately heavy dose of core consumers. The core consumer is more likely to step forward and respond to surveys about the

product or service in question, whereas the fringe user elects not to bother with it.

So how do you identify the wants and needs of the elusive fringe? You take the same wants and needs of your core, then you simplify. Make it easier to buy, easier to use. Make it so convenient your fringe will buy and use with little effort.

This is exactly how America Online became so successful. They appeal to the fringe internet user by making it simple and easy, yet they satisfy the same needs and wants of the core internet user (such as e-mail and access to all kinds of information). Apple did the same with the Macintosh computer. In fact, Apple has two lines of Macintoshes, the heavy-duty, cutting-edge, "high end" line for the core user, and the iMac line for the fringe user.

- **Step 3: Craft different ads for your core and fringe.** Ads targeted to your core can contain detailed information, hitting numerous features and benefits (of course, some mediums are more conducive to this than others). Ads targeted to your fringe should be short and sweet, and emphasize one main benefit (hint: ease of use or convenience).

- **Step 4: Use different media outlets to reach your core and fringe.** Buy highly targeted media for your core ads and more mass appeal media for your fringe ads.

- **Step 5: Use The Sprinkler Strategy.** A rotating water sprinkler wets the entire lawn by spraying water in only one direction at a time, but constantly changing direction at the same time. You can do the same with your advertising and promotions.

Shoot some ads in the direction of your core. Then pivot and do a fringe promotion. Then pivot and shoot some ads in the direction of your fringe. Then pivot again and do a core promotion. Keep pivoting and keep mixing it up. You can overlap many selected ad runs and/or promotions, running different ones concurrently, if you like.

This is not meant to sound like a haphazard or unplanned approach. Using *The Sprinkler Strategy,* you can have a well-planned, well-orchestrated marketing program in effect. It will keep you attentive to the various needs and wants of your core and fringe elements. As long as you constantly pivot, and don't ignore one element long enough for it to get "dry," you'll maximize impact and be well on your way to creating massive demand!

Chapter Twelve

Direct Mail Deployment

Many demand-creating techniques are implemented through advertising in various media outlet types, such as radio, television, magazines, newspapers, billboards, etc. As you've noticed, I've been explaining how to implement in these media outlet types as we've been going along. But there's one media outlet type that warrants its own chapter.

Because of the unique attributes of direct mail*, it is very conducive to many of our demand-creating techniques. Also, it's becoming very popular with many marketers that have their own databases going. Unfortunately, direct mail is often misunderstood and misused. You need to be able to take full advantage of direct mail, and you need to reduce your chances of misusing it. You will accomplish both with this chapter.

---

*I'm talking about regular old fashioned direct mail, not e-mail. While you could apply most of this chapter to e-mail, you must be very cautious. "Spamming" people with unwanted e-mail advertising elicits much greater anger and animosity than snail mail does.

DIRECT MAIL MISCONCEPTIONS

First let's clear up some popular myths about direct mail advertising.

- **Myth: It's "junk mail" — people don't read it.**

  Truth: People read their mail. I guarantee, if I sent you a letter, you'd open it and read it. The same would happen if you sent me one. "But you're talking about a personal letter," you say. "What about a printed advertising piece?"

  The only reasons a person does not open and read an advertising piece are that (*a*) they already know what it's about, and (*b*) they already know they're not interested at the present time. No different than with any other form of advertising, in which only a small percent of the receivers respond each time an ad runs.

  Notice that when someone receives an advertising piece in the mail that interests them, they consider it valuable information, not "junk mail." Only the stuff that doesn't interest them at the moment is trashed. Then again, the majority of all advertising is mentally and/or physically trashed by the recipients. (You don't see people recording radio or television commercials, or clipping couponless ads from magazines or newspapers, just to save them, do you?) Trashed advertising comes with the territory, no matter what media outlet types you use.

  By and large, people enjoy receiving mail (except for bills, perhaps). For every one person who complains about being on some mailing list, five other people sign up to receive product or service information in the mail. Receiving mail is a delightful experience. Want proof? Watch how quickly people fetch their mail after it arrives. And when people come home from work, what's one of the first things they like to do?

- **Myth: People don't respond to direct mail.**

  Truth: People respond exceptionally well to direct mail. People fill out, return, clip, sniff, call phone numbers . . . whatever. Direct mail is a aggressive, intrusive advertising vehicle. It can motivate people to act and act quickly.

  Direct mail, like all advertising, is subject to "the numbers." The more pieces you mail out, the more response you'll get.

But it's also subject to a number of seemingly inconsequential details which turn out to be anything but inconsequential in affecting response rate. Later in this chapter, I'll offer four simple tips that you can use to boost your response rate significantly.

- **Direct mail is very expensive.**

Truth: All advertising is expensive. However, like all other media, there are ways to do direct mail economically.

A small business can direct mail to 10,000 or more households in their immediate trading area for only a few hundred dollars with a "shared" mailer such as Val-Pak. ("Shared" means the costs of the mailing are divided among the many businesses whose pieces are all contained in the envelope or booklet mailed.) Compared with most other advertising vehicles, we're talking dirt cheap here. Yet the response can be very good.

Even a full-color, elaborate piece can be mailed reasonably, if you know what you're doing. Your per-piece printing cost drops appreciably at certain quantities, usually between 50,000 and 500,000. Additional savings can occur if you keep your piece "letter size" (which is actually much larger than your typical #10 letter envelope). Additional savings occur when your addresses are carrier route pre-sorted, and if you mail to at least 90 percent of all the addresses in each Zip Code, and if you use Zip+Four.

You can also hit your core consumers or prospects relatively inexpensively when you maintain an in-house database. More on this later.

THE ADVANTAGES OF DIRECT MAIL

Direct mail is very conducive to implementing many of our demand-creating techniques. Here's what you can accomplish with direct mail:

- **Interact with your core.** Direct mail can be targeted precisely to the people you desire. It's great for working your core. Remember, your core likes detailed information and values communication from you.

- **Reach your fringe.** The fringe is, by nature, rather elusive. Your fringe may not step out of the shadows and communicate with you, but you can step forward and communicate with them. Not everyone reads the publications, watches the television shows, or drives by the billboards you advertise in. But everyone must live somewhere, and that somewhere has an address. With direct mail, you can reach into the depths of the marketplace and hit potential buyers you never knew existed.

- **Persuade in detail.** The written word can be very commanding. While long copy is often undesirable in newspaper and magazine ads, it often works well in direct mail pieces.

- **Support your other media runs.** The CBS television network, like other networks, uses its own airtime to promote upcoming shows and advertises in *TV Guide* and selected newspapers. But did you know they also direct mail to various types of people who may have a special interest in a particular show? One "48 Hours" show, for example, dealt with the advertising industry, so CBS bought a mailing list of advertising people and shot out notices.

- **Mobilize people.** The Grateful Dead built themselves into a legendary band, with a huge following, by touring. And everywhere they performed, tickets would be sold out for weeks in advance, even before the media heard about the scheduled event. How did this happen? The Dead maintained a database of hundreds of thousands of people, and mailed to them regularly, keeping them apprised of each upcoming concert and selling them tickets well in advance.

  Why wouldn't a web site work just as well? When you require people to be proactive and seek you out, you may be disappointed. Direct mail, on the other hand, is intrusive; it's a water-in-the-face splash that gets their attention and gets them to act now.

  When your sales are geared around a specific event or time period, you may do well to augment your other media buys with a direct mail notice.

- **Expose without display.** When you purchase exposure in most media outlet types — radio, television, newspaper, magazine, billboard, etc. — your ads are "out there" for everyone and anyone to see. That, of course, is what you want. Or perhaps naked display is not exactly what you want. There may be times when you prefer that your competitors and all the world not be exposed to your marketing. In a later chapter you're going to see that there are times when you do not want certain types of people to see your advertising. You still, however, want to achieve the kind of high impact exposure that a mass medium provides. Direct mail is your answer. That's why many marketers call direct mail their "secret weapon."

- **Make multiple impact.** One single direct mail piece can produce benefits which ripple on and on.

First, you achieve *frontal impact* when your pieces first hit mailboxes and make their initial impression on the recipients.

Next, you achieve *participating impact* as people see your piece many times during the period in which your piece is "alive" or "active." I'm referring mainly to pieces designed around a contest that keeps people playing for a number of weeks. Or pieces that contain multiple coupons with staggered and consecutive validation dates. Or pieces that contain a calendar of events, or some reference information.

Third, you get *residual impact* when people respond. Response may be in the form of a contest entry card or a product order blank the recipient has filled out and sent back. Or an order blank the recipient faxes back. Or an order placed by phone. Or the redemption of a coupon when the recipient physically trots into your store.

THE DUAL MAILING STRATEGY

You really should have two separate mailing programs in effect.

Program One: Do regular mailings to your core. Core-directed mailings should be done regularly, such as once per month or once per quarter. These are just a routine part of core maintenance.

Luckily, we live in a time where there are inexpensive computers and excellent database programs or contact management software readily available. You should set up an in-house database if you haven't already done so. Build your database by collecting names and addresses of customers, or people who return recycling cards (explained in the next chapter), warranty registration cards, contest activator or entry cards, or product order forms.

Core mailings can be done with a purchased list, but if you mail to them regularly, you'd be better off maintaining your own list in the long run.

Program Two: Once or twice per year, do a major, high-profile, razzle-dazzle mailing to your core and fringe together. This is like net fishing. Your huge net sweeps the marketplace and rakes in all kinds of living organisms — most of whom have never dealt with you before. The purpose of a core+fringe mailing is to recruit new customers and to inspire people who are not currently buying your product or service to sample you. You will find that a well-conceived, well-executed direct mail campaign is an excellent customer recruitment tool.

To do an effective core+fringe mailing, you must purchase a mailing list from a list company to augment your own list. Your own database alone will not do, since the object is to reach people who are not currently buying your product or service (or who may never even have heard of you before).

"WHAT DO I MAIL?"

A client radio station once spent several weeks setting up a database system and entering names and addresses of previous contest entrants. After they'd entered over 7,000 names and were ready to print their first batch of labels, it suddenly occurred to them they had no idea what they should mail to these people. A letter of some sort? A newsletter? A contest piece? What?

Since summer was approaching and a number of their air personalities would soon be taking vacations, I jokingly suggested they mail postcards from exotic locations signed by the disc jockeys. I then offered my real suggestions, which weren't quite so flamboyant. A few weeks later the general manager sent me copies of a postcard . . . with a full-color photo of the morning guy pulling some kind of fish out of the water, each grinning from ear to ear (fin to fin, in the fish's case). The reverse side had a handwritten note asking people to "keep listenin' while I'm fishin'."

There's no limit to what you mail when you think creatively! Use your imagination and be playful, fun, intriguing. However, there are some key ingredients that an effective direct mail piece should contain. Let's explore that now.

For Regular, Core-Directed Mailings

Your piece can take any shape or size that you like. But make sure it contains some or all of these attributes:

- **A "personal" letter or note.** Make it from someone in charge — the owner, CEO, president, or manager.
- **A coupon.** Coupons are, and will continue to be, a valuable part of marketing. When you issue a coupon worth $1 off (or, say $200 off a big-ticket item), you've just handed the recipient real "money" with built-in incentive to "spend" it in the manner you, the marketer, dictate. The "use it or lose it" feeling can take over, and the buyer can feel compelled to redeem the thing. If you're looking for a simple, inexpensive incentive that can produce a major sales boost — especially repeat business — consider coupons.
- **Standard information about your business or product.** Prominently show your hours of business, location(s), phone number, e-mail and web addresses, product offerings, etc. As your piece takes on reference value, people are more likely to keep it.
- **Customer testimonials.** One of the primary functions of your regular core mailings is to reinforce the purchase decision. We'll talk more about reinforcement in Chapter 20. For now, just be aware that client testimonials are valuable.
- **Upcoming promotions or specials.** Pre-promote weeks or months in advance. The idea is to build core interest (or actual sales) in advance. Then, any fringe business you get is just frosting on that core cake.
- **A recycling card or certificate.** When you recycle your customers, you're providing incentive for them to buy or patronize more often and at different times or days. Recycling is an important technique that warrants detailed discussion, and you'll read more about it in the next chapter.

For Core+Fringe Mailings

The following key ingredients should be included in every major core+fringe mailing:

- **An order blank or coupon.** You want to recruit new customers or clients, right? Then you need to provide them with a vehicle with which to respond. With a well-designed, clean looking order blank or coupon, your response rate will increase.
- **Persuasive copy.** Beyond simply recruiting new patronage, your ultimate goal is to maintain that patronage for a long time hence. You need to influence, convince, and motivate people. And a great way to do this is with some well-written, strong, persuasive copy.

In some of your core+fringe mailings, though perhaps not all, you may want to include the following:

- **A contest.** The two primary objectives of a contest are to catch new customers or patrons who otherwise wouldn't respond, and to increase or extend patronage of your existing or former customers. A well-conceived, well-executed contest accomplishes these objectives.
- **An entry blank or activator card.** When the recipient fills out an "activator card" or entry blank and returns it (via mail, fax, e-mail, or in person), the recipient has committed to some form of subsequent action. In other words, he makes one decision — submitting the entry form — then subsequently acts in accordance with that decision by returning to your store each week to see which card has been drawn, or tuning in to your commercial to see if his name is announced, or to build up "points" or chances to win.

  With an activator card or entry blank, you reduce many recurring decisions, such as where to eat lunch each day, to one decision followed by corroborating actions. This is a great way to create buying habits.
- **A winning number.** A five- or six-digit number printed on a game piece is an alternative to an activator card or entry blank. (Participants compare their numbers with those drawn and designated as winners.) However, a winning number doesn't

prompt patronage commitment so strongly as an activator card or entry blank. In addition, you cannot collect names for your database with a winning number-type contest. But you can still run a good contest and recruit new patronage, which may be your primary objective.

HOW TO INCREASE RESPONSE RATE

When people receive a direct mail piece, they run it through a series of mental questions, or hurdles, in search of appropriate answers (usually this happens subconsciously, and very fast). As your piece answers each successive question, the piece moves along the road of influence, gaining value in the recipient's mind as it advances. When your piece fails to answer a question, or clear a hurdle, it stops advancing and is rejected at that point and has no further effect.

Your objective is to answer all of the following questions. You achieve that by designing your piece with the answers in prominent display. Because the recipient's mind likes to make lightning-fast decisions about your piece, you can't afford to hide these attributes. The easier to see and grasp, the more effective your piece will be.

- **Question number one: "Who is sending this to me?"** Identify yourself as the sender, clearly and boldly. Some direct mailers believe the more nebulous or deceptive the outside of their piece appears, specifically regarding the true identity of the sender, the more impact and response it generates. While you may trick the recipient into opening the piece, as some marketers do with pieces that appear to be sent from some governmental agency, you ultimately hurt yourself by doing so. Hit-and-run marketers that rely on direct mail deception may realize a short-term blip in response, but consequently suffer much greater long-term failure. Legitimate marketers need and strive for long-term customer satisfaction and repeat business, neither of which is achieved by tricking people.
- **Question number two: "What do I get from this?"** Give them the bottom line payoff, what you are proposing and how they benefit from it. If you elect to provide detailed information, fine. But don't require the recipient to read through all the de-

tails to figure out what you're offering or what they're going to get out of it.

- **Question number three: "What's it gonna cost me?"** Once again, state it clearly and prominently.
- **Question number four: "What do I do next?"** Lead the recipient by the hand, tell them exactly what you'd like them to do next. "Fill out the entry card and mail it back," "Come to our store this weekend," "Call 555-345-6789 now," are examples. I'm suggesting the same writing style that appears in board games in which a player picks up a card that tells him exactly what to do next (as in "Advance to Go and collect $200").

PART 4

LEVERAGING DEMAND

When you *leverage demand*, you're spreading demand to the masses — reaching and affecting hundreds, thousands, or millions of people. But leveraging is much more than simply spreading. When you leverage demand, you implement specific techniques that are *self-replicating* in nature. That is, once you have set your demand-leveraging systems in motion, demand then *spreads itself*, ultimately producing double, triple, or even 10 times the results you would otherwise realize! Leveraging demand is like pouring oil onto water. The oil spreads itself far and wide without any further effort on your part. This is the real secret to creating major demand. This is what shoots your demand jet to its highest altitude.

Each of the seven chapters in this part contains extremely powerful and effective demand-leveraging techniques. Some require such a low financial and manpower investment on your part they may appear weak or inconsequential. Do not be fooled by the deceptively simple nature of these demand-creating techniques we are about to discuss. Simplicity is part of their beauty, not to mention their budget-friendly nature, which I'm sure you can appreciate.

Chapter Thirteen

Get Them to Buy More, More Often, through Recycling

We'll start with one of the simplest demand leveraging techniques, *recycling*. Recycling techniques are extremely simple and easy to implement. In fact, you may be tempted to pass them up, thinking something so simple cannot produce a worthwhile result. I assure you, however, that the demand you create with simple recycling techniques will be well in excess of your investment in them.

THE RECYCLING CONCEPT

The idea behind recycling is to generate more purchases from your existing consumers, customers, or clients. When you coax a customer into buying again sooner, or buying another related product, or buying a different time of day or time of year than she would without your coaxing, you're recycling your customer. Recycling is a proactive, rather than a reactive, process. You proactively recycle your customer by implementing certain recycling techniques. You don't just sit back and hope they buy again someday.

To recycle your customers, you must set things up so that each purchase is not an end in itself, but is the *first step toward the next purchase.* From the consumer's viewpoint, the purchase of your product or service provides a linkage to the next purchase, as when two people out on a date make plans to get together for a subsequent date.

Nightclub Example

As you know, the nightclub business is very trendy and cliquish. People can flock habitually to one place on one night of the week and to another nightclub on another night of the week (preferring to be wherever things are "happening" on any given night). The nightclub in this example had a great turnout every Wednesday night. In fact, it was well known for being "the place to be" on Wednesday nights. But Friday nights were another story. For whatever reason, Friday night was sparse.

Here's how the nightclub became packed on Friday nights in less than three weeks after instituting a recycling program. On one Wednesday night, they handed each patron who came through the door a special "VIP Card." The credit card-sized card offered free admission for two on Friday night before 10 P.M. (the club normally charged a $2 cover). In addition, the card could be redeemed for one free drink on Friday night.

The result? A good number of people from the Wednesday night crowd came back on Friday night. It took only two Wednesday nights of recycling to produce an overflow crowd on Friday nights.

It worked so well, they went the next logical step and printed up different VIP Cards, on different colored stock, for use on different nights. On some Fridays, for example, they'd pass out cards that were good for Tuesday nights; on some Tuesdays they'd pass out cards that were good for Thursday nights.

There are some very specific design elements you must use to make your recycling program work. Let's analyze how this nightclub used those key elements.

- **Good on a subsequent visit.** To cash in on the card's value, the recipient had to physically return to the nightclub on another night of the week.
- **One card, two free admissions.** By making each recycling card good for free admission for two, they encouraged each cardholder to bring someone (this is also an example is the *encouraged endorsement* technique we'll cover in the next chapter). This is how you can virtually double your business overnight!
- **Time deadline.** By making the free admission good only before 10 P.M., they encouraged people to get there relatively early. This accomplished two very important objectives. First, it headed people off who would otherwise have gone to another nightclub initially. Second, it got the place packed early, giving the later arrivals the impression the place was crowded and therefore the place to be.
- **Free bonus.** The free drink redemption value also accomplished three important objectives. First, it gave the cardholder a reason to stay for a while rather than just cruise through and leave as fast as they came (presuming it takes time to consume a drink). Second, it jump-started the bar as the arrivals went straight there to redeem the card before the 10 P.M. deadline. Third, it boosted bar sales quickly, as each person bought a drink for their friend when they redeemed the card for their own drink (notice each card was good for *one* free drink, not two as with admission.)
- **Card must be redeemed.** Cardholders used their card as a coupon when getting their free drink. In other words, they had to turn it in, use it like cash. To get another card, they'd have to come back another night. Or, if they were handed a new card when they arrived that night, they would have to come another night to redeem the new one.

Other Examples

The dry cleaner I go to recycles me with a "Special Customer Card." Each time I have shirts laundered, the clerk punches a hole in another number on the card, representing the number of shirts I had cleaned. When the number 50 is reached, I redeem the card to have three shirts laundered at no charge.

I know an auto service center that issues a card containing the numbers one through five. Each time you get your oil changed, they sign by another number. After five paid changes, you can redeem the card for a sixth oil change on the house.

After purchasing something from a household furnishings mail-order marketer, I received a card good for $10 off my next purchase.

Broadcasters use recycling techniques all the time. Radio and television stations and networks are constantly cross-promoting different dayparts or shows. This means the morning shows are asking you to tune in to the afternoon shows. And the afternoon shows are asking you to turn in to the evening shows. And the evening shows are asking you to tune in the next morning. And on and on.

McDonald's runs their Monopoly contest almost every spring. With each contest piece you acquire, not only could you be an instant winner of a small prize such as a cheeseburger, fries, or drink, but you could become a big winner of a major prize by accumulating game pieces that make up a complete set, such as all four railroads. You must keep returning to McDonald's to accumulate game pieces, of course.

Equity in a Subsequent Purchase

Notice that recycling not only can inspire customers to buy more and/or more often, but it can also reduce the chances of them patronizing a competitor. When you recycle, you're giving your clients an *equity interest* in a subsequent purchase. Suddenly your product or service is more valuable than a competitor's , since the buyer now possesses some equity in yours. Who wants to throw away equity? The old "use it or lost it" reasoning takes hold once again, and the buyer favors you over a competitor with which he has no equity.

THE IMPORTANCE OF RECYCLING

If you let someone purchase your product or service without getting a recycling card into their hands, you're forfeiting future business. Conversely, every time you get a recycling card into the hands of a consumer or customer, you're increasing the odds of that person buying again. Get a lot of recycling cards out and your sales can bloat dramatically.

Are you sometimes disheartened by the fact that consumers sometimes view your competitors' products so similar to yours that they don't seem to care which brand they buy? One brand can be just as good as the next to some people. What makes a consumer with no strong brand preference suddenly adopt a strong brand preference? Equity in a subsequent purchase will do it. And what provides that equity? A recycling card. It make so much sense and costs so little to implement, you should never be without a good recycling program in effect at all times.

HOW TO IMPLEMENT RECYCLING

As you can see, recycling is not difficult to implement. If you follow these four steps, and include the key elements outlined on page 145, you'll have recycling working for you in no time.

- **Step 1: Determine what specific behavior you wish to occur.** Would you like your customers to buy again within the week, month, or year? Would you like them to purchase a related product or service? You must be specific. "I would like them to buy our brand again the next time they need toothpaste," is too general. "I would like them to buy our deodorant within 60 days of buying our toothpaste" is better.

- **Step 2: Provide equity in a subsequent purchase.** The first thing that may come to mind is to offer a monetary discount (i.e., "$1 off your next purchase"). That's okay, but not quite so strong as offering a bonus product or service.

  Your product or service itself is a great source of equity. The nightclub I talked about earlier offered two free Friday night admissions plus a free drink to each Wednesday night patron. The free admissions and drink are the equity. They could have offered a $5 discount instead, but that doesn't sound quite as enticing.

- **Step 3: Make it tangible.** It's not enough to ask people to buy again verbally or in print. You must literally put your recycling offer into their hands. This means you must make it tangible. Create a recycling card or certificate. Give it a prestigious name like "VIP Card" or "Special Customer Card." Make sure the equity you're offering is stated clearly on the card.

  Another way to make your recycling tangible is to add equity to something that is already tangible, as McDonald's does with their Monopoly game pieces. By making each piece part of a winning set, each piece takes on extra value. This makes it much more valuable than a plain old coupon. If you already own Boardwalk, aren't you motivated to get Park Place too, so you can win a million dollars?!

- **Step 4: Distribute your recycling card at the time of purchase (or delivery).** Remember, to recycle people you must make each purchase the first step toward the next purchase. Making recycling-type offers in your ads or commercials is not recycling. Nor is indiscriminately passing out your recycling cards on the street corner. To procure a recycling card, a person must make a purchase. Chain-link them so one purchase leads to the next.

Chapter Fourteen

Turn Customers into Persuaders

The idea is to inspire your consumers, customers, or clients to recruit new consumers, customers, or clients — like a church or civic organization whose members actively recruit new members. Like the nightclub we discussed in the last chapter that made each recycling card good for free admission for two, thus encouraging the cardholder to bring a friend.

The technique is called *encouraged endorsement.* It comes about as you, the marketer, encourage your customers to endorse you. When you encourage endorsement of your product, service, or business, you are empowering each of your customers to assist you in the demand creation process. It's as though you "deputize" your customers and make them pseudo-members of your sales staff.

You can encourage your customers to endorse either aggressively or passively. Each works differently, so we'll discuss them separately, beginning with aggressive endorsement.

ENCOURAGED AGGRESSIVE ENDORSEMENT

Aggressive endorsement occurs when one person persuades another to patronize your establishment, or to buy your product or service. In this sense, aggressive endorsement can also be called recommendation. Here are some examples:

A lawnmower marketer offered a $25 limited-time rebate on a particular model. The buyer was required to fill out and return a special rebate card (another way of collecting names for the database). The rebate card was perforated down the middle so it could be torn in half, producing two smaller cards. The buyer was instructed to return one of the cards to get the rebate, and to give the other card to someone who might be in the market for a new lawnmower. Here's the actual wording that appeared on the second card: "Know a friend, neighbor, or relative who could use a new Acme lawnmower? Do him of her a favor. Give them this card, good for a $25 rebate on a brand new Acme lawnmower." Notice the copy asks the person to deliberately recommend the Acme brand by giving the card to someone.

Columbia House record club sends its members a pamphlet with this offer: Sign up a friend and you get three CDs or four cassette tapes for free. Part of the pamphlet is a membership application; fill in your friend's name, tear the card off at the perforation, and mail it in. Actually, there are two membership applications provided, in case you want to get six CDs or eight cassettes free by signing up two friends.

How did America Online sign up so many members so fast? They encouraged each member to recommend AOL to a friend in exchange for free hours.

Geico Insurance sends its policy holders a pamphlet with this heading: "Why should YOU help your friends to save more with GEICO?" It then provides reasons for doing so. It even has a three-panel cartoon showing one person giving the pamphlet (which contains an application form), to a neighbor.

Two earlier examples also fall into the aggressive endorsement category: the organization that encourages its members to recruit others, and the nightclub that passes out recycling cards encouraging each recipient to bring a friend or date when returning on another night. (Recycling and encouraged endorsement work well together. Often you can implement both techniques with one card.)

ENCOURAGED PASSIVE ENDORSEMENT

Passive endorsement occurs when a person displays use of a particular product or service. They key word is display. The display of usage is seen by others, who are in turn influenced to choose that particular brand. If you encourage properly, your customers will be passively endorsing your product automatically, without making any deliberate recommendation.

One of the best examples of passive endorsement can be seen on the back of every pickup truck. Just about every pickup manufacturer puts the company or brand name on the tailgate. And not just painted on, but embossed in the metal. And not in small letters, but in huge letters that stretches across the entire width of the vehicle. When you buy a pickup truck, you're displaying the make you've chosen for all to see, every minute you're on the road and every minute it's parked in your driveway. Kind of makes you want to send good ol' Ford, Chevrolet, or Toyota a bill for your endorsement services, doesn't it?

Many clothing marketers encourage passive endorsement by making sure their logos are prominently visible on their products. Lacoste's alligator, Polo's polo player, Levi's pocket tag, Nike's swoosh, and Tommy Hilfiger's name are a few examples.

Clothing is a great vehicle for encouraging passive endorsement even if you're not a clothing marketer. I have a line of high-quality polo shirts with my logo (which is my name in signature form) embroidered on them, and people wear them all the time. The fact that my name is not as well know as, say, Tommy Hilfiger's, is an added bonus for me. When someone asks the wearer, "Who's Rick Ott?", the wearer goes from a passive endorser to an aggressive endorser when he or she answers the question.

Notice that passive endorsement is much more than simple logo exposure. When a client displays her usage, she is implying support; she is putting her personal "stamp of approval" on your product. It's not the name "FORD" on your tailgate that does the trick;

it's you, driving the Ford in public, showing your support, that makes the difference. You needn't be any kind of celebrity, either. Your friends and co-workers know you personally, which says enough to them. Strangers see the way you look, the way you come across, and that tells them what type of people to associate with that product. Passive endorsement carries much greater influence power than simple logo exposure.

WHY PEOPLE ENDORSE

Why would a person want to endorse a product or service? Asked another way, what incentive is needed to get a person to aggressively or passively endorse your product or service?

A person will engage in endorsement activity for any of the following reasons:

- **To gain higher status.** The endorser displays his allegiance to a particular product or service as a means of bonding with the type of people the product or service represents. He wants the status to transfer from the product to himself, as happens when he pulls out a 24-carrot gold Cross pen in the presence of others.

  Also, an endorser may rise in status by appearing knowledgable and experienced. An act of aggressive endorsement puts the endorser in an elevated position in the eyes of the person he's talking to (or so he believes).

- **To share experiences.** It's instinctive for humans to want to share experiences. We want others to experience that which we find pleasurable.

- **To gain reinforcement.** People don't always feel confident with every purchase decision they make. One way a person gains positive reinforcement regarding a recent purchase is to recommend the same item to another. If the other person sees value in it and buys, it makes the first person feel better about her purchase.

Now that you know why people are motivated to endorse, you can encourage it with the proper incentives.

HOW TO ENCOURAGE AGGRESSIVE ENDORSEMENT

- **Step 1: Create an endorsement card or pamphlet.** An endorsement card is similar to a recycling card. In fact, a single card can be both a recycling card and an endorsement card if the card contains both recycling and endorsing elements. Like recycling, aggressive endorsement occurs much more often when you use a tangible card or pamphlet.
- **Step 2: Use wording that inspires the recipient to aggressively endorse.** More than likely, people will need an incentive to recommend your product or service. The best incentives you can offer satisfy the buyer's need to gain status, share experiences, or have their purchase decision reinforced.

  Geico's pamphlet encourages aggressive endorsement by pointing out the great favor you'll be performing when you help your friend save money on his automobile insurance. That's the gaining status motive.

  Here are two examples that play on the sharing of experiences:

  "SPECIAL PATRON TICKET. Free soft drink, coffee, or tea with any dinner purchase. Treat yourself and a guest to the extraordinary Maria's Kitchen experience. Valid any Monday after 6 P.M. during the month of June."

  "Double your fun! Take a friend along next time you visit your favorite Acme Toy dealer. When you buy two or more of the same accessory, we'll give you each $2 off!"

  Here's one that uses reinforcement as the main incentive:

  "One of the greatest benefits to owning Krater brand carpeting is seeing how others enjoy its superb feel and decorative beauty when they visit. When anyone asks, or pays you a compliment, as they undoubtedly will, be sure to tell them it's Krater Carpeting they're enjoying. Pass along the attached card as well. It will entitle the recipient to use the same ONE FREE ROOM OF PADDING you received. Smart homeowners like you choose Krater when they want the very best."

- **Step 3: Include an encouraged endorsement card with every**

item purchased. Or send the card out with your next core-directed database mailing.

HOW TO ENCOURAGE PASSIVE ENDORSEMENT

- **The one and only step: Attach your logo to your product in a highly visible position.** It does you little good to have people buying and using your product if other people cannot instantly determine it's your product they're using. It's up to you to make sure your logo is visible. Passive endorsement is not going to happen if you leave it up to the customer to seek out your logo and display it somehow.

  (Throughout this book I've offered various tips to pull a commodity item out of the quagmire, and this is another one. Attach a logo to a commodity item, and the item is no longer such a commodity. That's exactly how generic blue jeans became unique designer jeans. And how Chiquita differentiated its bananas from other brands.)

  How do you attach a logo to a service? It's a bit more difficult than with a product, but there are ways. Construction companies will often put a large sign in front of the site they're building to let the public know it's them at work. Chemlawn parks its flashy truck in front of your house for all your neighbors to see.

  Some services are not conducive to encouraged endorsement because people do not want it known they're using certain services. Not many people would be willing to walk around wearing a sticker on their jackets displaying the name "Dr. Joe Doe — Plastic Surgery," for example.

  Although I maintain fairly high visibility as a professional speaker and author, I'm forced to conduct actual consulting services in a low profile, clandestine fashion sometimes. Few people want it known they're bringing in a management or marketing consultant (other than for a speaking engagement), and virtually no one will display any such usage. If your service is not conducive to usage display, you may find it difficult to encourage endorsement. But if you do invent a way, let me know.

Chapter Fifteen

Magically Attract People to Your Product or Service

You're going to enjoy this chapter. It deals with the essence of human behavior, why consumers choose the products and services they do. We'll examine how people are subconsciously attracted to certain products and services, and how people are likewise repelled by other products and services. And we'll see how people influence others to behave in the same manner.

With this information, you will be able to harness human influence and behavior and begin making it work for you in a major way. You will be able to cause people to become irresistibly attracted to your product, service, or business. You will learn how to avoid inadvertently repelling buyers — something very few marketers understand. It really is magical in the way it happens, and you're going to discover the secrets to it all right now.

The first step is to gain an understanding of the two keys that control human influence and behavior: The Style, Art, and Fashion Factor, and Influence Types. Let's start with the former.

THE STYLE, ART, AND FASHION (SAF) FACTOR

Human influence is most acute and visible in the area of *style, art, and fashion*, or *SAF*. The *SAF Factor* plays a very important role in the entire human behavioral process, which will become evident as this discussion unfolds.

Some products and services are *SAF-intensive*. This means they inherently have a lot to do with style, art, and fashion. Examples include, but are not limited to, clothing, home furnishings, automobiles, beauty aids, music, magazines, hair styling and grooming supplies, radio stations, restaurants, etc.

Other products and services are *SAF-light*, meaning they have inherently little to do with style, art, and fashion. Examples include, but are not limited to, life insurance, dry cleaning, fast food, accounting services, groceries, legal services, power tools, etc. However, *the marketing of any product, service, or business, whether it's SAF-intensive or SAF-light, has everything to do with style, art, and fashion.* Marketing is, by nature, SAF-intensive. In fact, advertising is a form of style, art, and fashion expression. You may be the manufacturer or retailer of an SAF-light item such as a pipe wrench, but when you market your pipe wrench, you're suddenly dealing with style, art, and fashion in a big way, whether you ever intended to be or not.

Make no mistake about it — the SAF Factor has everything to do with the success of your product, service, or business, regardless of your item's nature.

INFLUENCE TYPES

We human beings are constantly influencing one another to behave in the same manner as we behave. Most of this human-to-human adoptive influence happens subconsciously. Without realizing it, you are being influenced to do what you see other people doing, or to say what you hear other people saying. Likewise, you are influencing others to do as you do and repeat what you say. In the real world, it is human see, human do.

While we are all alike in that we are constantly both influencing others and being influenced by others, we differ from one another in our *receptivity of newness* as it relates to style, art, and fashion. In other words, some people are very receptive to new style, art, and fashion, and adopt quickly behavior that displays this receptivity. Other people are averse to new style, art, and fashion and hang on to old, familiar SAF for a long time.*

All humans fall into one of four *Influence Types*, based on their receptivity to newness in the areas of style, art, and fashion.

As we discuss each, please keep in mind that we are not judging people or attaching any relative values to the four types. We attach no right or wrong, good or bad, values to these categories. The last thing the world needs is another measure that encourages prejudice based on differences among people, and I'm not about to supply one. I'm merely introducing a new measure by which marketers may distinguish among consumer preferences simply as a means of better serving the consumer. You must keep any personal biases out of this system to use it effectively.

Type One Consumers

Type One people are extremely aware of, and receptive to, new style, art, and fashion. Type Ones not only seek and welcome SAF newness, they often create it. They are very quick to adopt new behavior. Type Ones view themselves as people on the cutting edge, the trendsetters. They thrive on being different, and look to display their uniqueness in a variety of ways. Type Ones constitute about 10 percent of the population.

---

*You must understand exactly what *new* or *newness* means in the SAF area. If you buy a brand new suit, yet the suit is a very traditional design and similar to other suits that have been worn by people for years, you are not displaying newness. But if the suit is the latest style and looks significantly different from most other suits, it's new. If you purchase a painting by an artist whose work appears very similar to that of other established artists, you are displaying a very low level of newness. If you purchase a painting from an artist whose work appears vastly different from anything else out there, you are displaying a high level of SAF newness. SAF newness is not necessarily that which never existed before. If wide ties, short skirts, or bell-bottom jeans have been dormant for a number of years, and then you begin wearing them, you're displaying newness, even though wide ties, short skirts, and bell bottoms have existed before. Style, art, and fashion trends come and go and circle around again and again over the years, you know.

Type Two Consumers

Like Type Ones, Type Twos are also receptive to style, art, and fashion newness. But unlike Type Ones, who naturally gravitate to the latest, Type Twos find their receptivity to style, art, and fashion newness somewhat strained. They have to put effort forth to maintain an awareness of the latest style, art, and fashion, but they do so because the effort is enjoyable. They also wait for the Type Ones to adopt some style, art, and fashion behavior for a while before they adopt. Once Type Twos adopt, however, they can perpetuate a trend fairly early. Type Twos constitute about 20 percent of the population.

Type Three Consumers

Unlike Types One and Two who actively seek and display SAF newness, Type Threes exert minimal effort. Their awareness of SAF newness is lower, and that's fine with them. Type Threes do not believe it is up to them to reach out and embrace style, art, and fashion newness. Instead, they wait for style, art, and fashion newness to reach them eventually, once its worked its way through the Ones and Twos. Type Threes only feel comfortable adopting something that has been around for a while, something they've grown familiar with over time. Which means by the time Type Threes adopt, its a much lower level of newness. Type Threes are a whopping 40 percent of the population.

Type Four Consumers

Type Fours are very averse to SAF newness. They don't want it, don't need it. Most of the time they're oblivious to style, art, and fashion newness because they limit their exposure to it. Type Fours are very slow to let go of old style, art, and fashion. Only after something has been around for quite a while do Type Fours begin adopting. By that time, it's a relatively low level of newness. Type Fours are about 30 percent of the population.

IDENTIFYING INFLUENCE TYPE

To begin harnessing the power of human influence, you must develop the ability to equate people with Influence Type. You must have a feel for what Influence Type category people fall into. This will enable you to determine the Influence Type(s) of your own consumers or customers, as well as the Type(s) you might wish to attract.

The primary way to ascertain Influence Type is through constant observation. Remember, the SAF Factor is the underlying determinant. How readily people accept newness of style, art, and fashion indicates what Influence Type they are. Display of SAF newness — high, low, or in-between — is what you're looking for. Here are the particulars:

Appearance is the most obvious Influence Type indicator. Clothing, hairstyle, and accessories (including glasses, if they are worn) can tell you a lot. Note people's entertainment preferences — the music or recording artists they like, the movies they prefer, the magazines they read. The type of car they drive, the way their home is decorated, and the restaurants they frequent are also tip-offs.

Gender, race, intelligence level, and age are irrelevant, though with the latter it might appear otherwise. As people age, the form in which they express their SAF preferences changes. A 20-year-old Type One might wear vastly different clothing from a 40-year-old Type One, who might wear vastly different clothing from a 60-year-old Type One. Also, people tend to drift in the One-to-Four direction as they get older. As people age, they put less effort forth to accept and adopt SAF newness. Of course, some people can do the opposite and move in the Four-to-One direction. They can reach a certain age and suddenly experience a personal renaissance, displaying a heightened awareness and adoption of SAF newness. But this is rare.

Despite the One-to-Four directional drift, the relative proportions of each Influence Type hold true in the aggregate, regardless of age (Ones, 10 percent; Twos, 20 percent; Threes, 40 percent; Fours, 30 percent). Thus the contention that Type Ones are the young people and Type Fours are the old people is false.

A couple cautions. Any one indicator may give you an inaccurate reading. While simply looking at someone's appearance will give you a general idea of where they fall, it's not a precise measure. Two or three different indicators may be needed to give you a more reliable measure of someone's Influence Type. (Keep in mind none of this is an exact science. It's subject to variance throughout.)

The worst way to ascertain Influence Type is to explain all this to someone and ask them what Type they believe they are. People almost always perceive themselves as hipper than they really are. So whatever Influence Type they say they are, you have to adjust accordingly. Also, despite cautions against doing so, people tend to instinctively attach values to the various Types. They can become defensive about where they fall, or even become saddened if you suggest they may be a different Type than what they perceive themselves to be.

THE SECRET TO MAGICAL ATTRACTION

It all boils down to four very important rules:

1. **Your product or service, combined with its marketing, is exuding some level of style, art, and fashion newness, either high or low.** In the case of SAF-light items, the marketing component carries the heavier load of style, art, and fashion. But regardless of which component — your product or your marketing — delivers what percentage of SAF, make no mistake about it: Your product and its marketing are telegraphing a certain level of SAF newness, high, low, or in-between.

2. **People are innately aware of the SAF nuances of every product or service and its marketing that they are exposed to.** This innate awareness is deeply subconscious most of the time.

3. **When your level of SAF newness matches a particular Influence Type, people of that Type are magically attracted.** It's as though you activated a "comfort button" in their brain. They feel your product or service is for them. The odds of them wanting and buying your item are very high.

4. **When your level of SAF newness mismatches a particular Influence Type, people of that Type are mysteriously repelled.** It's as though you set off a "discomfort button" in their brain. They feel your product or service is for people other than themselves, and the thought of buying it never enters their mind.

NEAT EXAMPLES

I'll bet there's a particular restaurant in your home town that you never go to. You have to admit the food may be fine, the prices reasonable, the service pretty good . . . yet you never go there. Or if you find yourself there one day because some friends or business acquaintances arranged a meeting, you notice yourself wanting to just grab a quick bite and get out. You don't stay any longer than you have to, and you have no desire to return.

Could it be that restaurant is exuding a level of SAF newness that mismatches your Influence Type? Could it be that restaurant made you feel uncomfortable in some way? (Now, you're analyzing this logically. But at the time, you just felt you didn't want to be in that restaurant, with no conscious thought about it.)

And how did you become subconsciously aware of that restaurant's SAF level? Did it have to do with the decor, including the use of wood versus metal or glass, the color of the walls and floor, the decorations? Did it have to do with the appearance of the other patrons? The appearance of the employees? Did it have to do with the background music, or the live entertainment? Of course, all these things and more contributed to that restaurant's SAF newness level.

What about the restaurant's location? It turns out different Influence Types feel comfortable with different sections of town. Type Ones like the heart of the city. They like to work there, live there, socialize there. Type Twos like the outskirts of the city. Type Threes, suburbia. Type Fours, the country. There are exceptions, but this is the prevailing behavior.

Perhaps that restaurant you don't like is located in a section of town that mismatches your Influence Type. And perhaps one of your favorite restaurants is located in a section of town that matches your

Influence Type. Incidently, restaurants should think about this before they choose a location. I've seen a fine Type Two-appeal restaurant go out of business because it was located in a Type Four section of town, and a fine Type Four-appeal restaurant fail because it was in a Type One-ish/Two-ish section of town.

The SAF Factor affects all businesses that have a physical location, not just restaurants. Walk into any department or discount store, furniture store, supermarket, hair salon, insurance office, whatever, and either your subconscious comfort button or discomfort button will be activated.

So You Want to Sell a House

Here's an interesting occurrence. A friend of mine was having a hard time selling her house. It was in fine shape, and the asking price was reasonable. Yet month after month went by, and while a good number of people were looking, no one was buying.

I took one look at the place and knew immediately what the problem was. The house was located in a Type Two section of town (within the city limits but not downtown), yet it exuded a low level of SAF newness.

"Paint the foyer and the living room walls purple," I suggested (they were a dull beige).

"Purple?!" she repeated somewhat incredulously.

"Actually, the name of the paint color is Periwinkle," I explained. "It's a vibrant, lavenderish purple."

Since she's a Type Three (in fact, close to a Four), she did not immediately see the wisdom in painting the walls Periwinkle. I had to use the Consultant's Oldest Line on her. "Just do it," I said on the way out. She wasn't any crazier about painting the walls Periwinkle after hearing the Consultant's Oldest Line, but when your explanation is only three words long, people do seem to pause and ponder.

A week or so later she called and said "I'm painting the walls Periwinkle. Are you sure this is going to work?" Sensing lingering doubt, I used the Consultant's Second Oldest Line, "Trust me."

A couple weeks later she called again, this time with a decidedly more upbeat demeanor. In fact, she was so excited she could hardly speak.

"You're not going to believe what happened," She exclaimed. "The first couple to see the house after I painted it bought . . . and they said they we're interested in the first 30 seconds! How could this happen?!"

You know what happened. Since the house was located in a Two-ish section of town, the odds were Type Twos would be looking to live there. We simply raised the house's level of SAF newness, by painting the first two rooms they would see upon entering Periwinkle. When the Type Twos entered, their comfort buttons were immediately activated; they felt the house was for them.

Incidently, the woman's brother, a solid Type Four, helped her with the painting, even though he expressed a strong opinion that "This ugly purple is ruining the house. Now no one will want it." (He was partially correct. No Type Four would want it. But Type Twos, and possibly Type Ones, would be attracted, as evidenced by the result.)

GETTING PERSONAL

I know this is a marketing book, but I'm going to take a minute to show you how the SAF Factor and Influence Types affect your personal life. Consider this a bonus section.

Take into consideration the SAF level of various items when it comes time to buy someone a gift. I once saw a Type Two couple give a Type Four couple a set of sleek, avant-garde candlestick holders. The Fours about gagged as they pulled them out of the box. And the Fours gave the Twos an equally mismatched gift. It was a set of coffee table coasters with a duck design. Let me tell you, if you want to make Type Twos (or Type Ones, for that matter) instantly nauseous, give them something with a duck on it.

A friend of mine once said he wouldn't be caught dead in a pair of Levi's Dockers. Even though he was 36 at the time, and in the bull's-eye of the product's target, his Influence Type did not match the SAF newness level exuded by Dockers and its marketing. (He's a Type Two, and Dockers are a portion of Three, but mainly Four.)

You and Your Significant Other

What Influence Type are you? What Type is your spouse or boyfriend/girlfriend? Do they match, or are the two of you mismatched? Here's what can happen under different arrangements:

If two people are the same Influence Type, chances are they'll feel a strong and deep level of comfort with one another. They'll probably agree on where to live, how the house should be decorated, how the kids should be dressed, what movies they want to see, etc. Each of you may find that the other seems to have some uncanny ability to bring out the best in you.

Let's say the two are different Influence Types, but adjacent. In other words, one is a Type One and the other a Type Two. Or a Type Two and a Type Three. Or a Type Three and a Type Four. One of them will be introducing newer style, art, and fashion behavior into the household, which shouldn't be a problem as long as they both understand what is happening. It's like a dance in which one person leads and the other follows. The adoption of newer behavior may spark some debate at times, but that's what keeps it interesting, in this scenario.

Let's say the two people are one Influence Type apart. A Type One and a Type Three, for example. Or a Type Two and a Type Four. The danger light is blinking on this one. I once observed a Type Two male grow increasingly dissatisfied with his relationship. He didn't know exactly why this dissatisfaction existed, because his girlfriend was, by his own admission, kind, caring, and committed. But he did notice they spent a lot of time arguing about the appropriateness of each other's dress, for one thing (she was a Type Four). They also disagreed about where they should go and what they should do quite often.

One day he met a new girl and felt an instant rapport, an instant bond of some kind. In a flash he backstroked out of the first relationship and dove effortlessly into the new one. She was a Type Two, same as him. They went everywhere together, they seemed to fire each other up with energy and enthusiasm. He did a happiness one-eighty.

What happens when a Type One and a Type Four get together? First of all, the odds are they wouldn't get together. Their worlds would simply never meet. But if they did get together somehow (blind date or the like), it wouldn't take long for each to accuse the other of being from another planet, and it'd be all over. I can't think of any examples of a One and a Four spending any meaningful time together.

HOW TO CAUSE PEOPLE TO BE MAGICALLY ATTRACTED TO YOUR PRODUCT OR SERVICE.

By now, you've got the idea. Here are the two main steps:

- **Step 1: Decide which Influence Type you want to appeal to.** Avoid the temptation to choose more than one. The wider your target, the trickier it becomes. (We'll discuss appealing to more than one Influence Type in the next chapter. For now, keep it simple and pick only one.)
- **Step 2: Design your marketing to match your targeted Influence Type.** You may have to raise or lower the SAF newness level of your marketing, or of the product itself.

Let me repeat: When your level of SAF newness matches a particular Influence Type, people of that Type are magically attracted. Match up, relax, and watch demand create before your very eyes!

Chapter Sixteen

Spread Demand Throughout the Population (or Your Target Market)

Human influence spreads via person-to-person contact, either directly or through the media. Relatives, friends, family members, acquaintances, co-workers, people on television, even strangers on the street are influencing one another all the time. You are being influenced by others all day, every day, whether you realize it or not. And you in turn are influencing others merely by what you do and say every day.

Think about this: Without human influence, almost no behavioral changes would ever occur. One person would arbitrarily adopt a new behavior, wearing a different style of shoe for example, and no one else would be influenced to do the same. The new shoe style would never catch on or spread. We'd all be dressing today the same as our ancestors did a couple hundred years ago (or for that matter, the way the Romans did thousands of years ago).

Human influence is a powerful, pervasive force that is affecting all things, including the success of your product, service, or business. Your sales are affected greatly by each person that influences another (or many others) either to buy your product or not. Thus *the level of demand for your product is being affected by human influence every minute of every day, including right now, in one way or another, whether you have anything to do with that influence or not.* Given that fact, it obviously behooves you to harness human influence and get it working for you, rather than ignoring it and accepting whatever consequence occurs.

If you enjoyed the last chapter, you're really going to love this one. We're going to take what we learned in Chapter 15 and build on it. We'll explore how adoptive influence travels through the population over time. You'll learn how your marketing and human influence work together to create demand. In fact, you'll learn exactly how to tap into the tremendous power of human influence to cause demand to spread wildly throughout the population (or your target market)!

THE INFLUENCE GRAPH

If it's been awhile since you read Chapter 15, you may want to review it now, since we're going to expand on that material here.

Remember Influence Types and how they differ from one another? Now, to further aid in harnessing human influence and spreading demand, let's graph the Influence Types. In Figure 2 you'll see each Influence Type placed side by side on what's called *The Influence Graph*.

The Influence Graph is a big-picture view of the population, bringing into play two very important elements that affect human influence: direction and time. Specifically, it shows how influence moves or flows from one Type to the next over time.

How The Influence Graph Works

Simply put, Type Ones influence the Type Twos; Type Twos influence Type Threes; Type Threes influence Type Fours. Adoptive in-

FIGURE 2
The Influence Graph

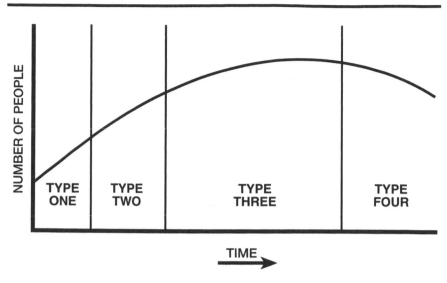

Influence travels from left to right over time.

fluence always moves from left to right through the population, never from right to left.

To illustrate how adoptive influence moves through the population, let's discuss a real-life example from the music industry. The behavior we'll examine is the purchase of musical product (CDs, tapes, posters, concert tickets) of the rock group U2.

In 1980 and '81, U2 was popular among Type Ones in the United States. The rest of the population hadn't even heard of U2 back then. Despite tremendous Type One acceptance, U2 sold a relatively small amount of product in the early '80s, since Type Ones represent only 10 percent of the total population.

As time went on and Type Ones displayed adoption of U2, Type Twos became influenced. Twos began buying U2 product, resulting in significantly greater sales by 1983. Up to this point, U2 received virtually no exposure on CHR (Contemporary Hit Radio) stations, and very little exposure on AOR (Album Oriented Rock) stations. However, MTV, which was targeting Type Ones and Twos at the time, embraced the band and gave them plenty of exposure. By 1984,

Type Two influence began to reach some Type Threes (those on the left side of the Type Three range). Once a recording artist crosses the line between the Type Two and Type Three ranges, the artist becomes "legitimate" as far as many mass-appeal radio stations are concerned. Thus in 1984 U2 began receiving some CHR airplay and a good amount of AOR airplay.

By 1987, when U2's album *The Joshua Tree* was released, the stage had been set for immediate Type Three acceptance. Mass-appeal radio stations jumped on it "out of the box." In fact, two songs from the CD became number one hits nationwide. As influence permeated throughout the Type Three range, sales of U2 product skyrocketed (remember, Type Threes are 40 percent of the population).

Toward the end of 1987, as U2 became one of the biggest bands in America, Type Fours began adopting. U2 product sales reached a peak around this time (Types Three and Four together are 70 percent of the population). By the fall of 1988, *The Joshua Tree* had sold over 5 million copies in the United States.

While U2's popularity was spreading throughout the Three and Four ranges, a very interesting consequence developed. The Ones began abandoning the band. As Type Ones are fond of saying, "If it sells, it smells," or "They (the artist) sold out." Why do the Ones feel this way? Type Ones, you will recall, feel they are the cutting-edge trendsetters. They take pride in their individuality and will associate with things that sets them apart from the masses. So when the masses adopt something, Type Ones feel compelled to disassociate to maintain their unique, trend-setting position.

Guess what? Not only does adoptive influence move through the population, but shunning influence moves through also. As Type Ones began shunning U2 in late 1987, they influenced Type Twos to do the same. U2's next CD, called *Rattle and Hum*, was purchased mainly by right-sided Threes and Type Fours, and didn't sell nearly as well as *The Joshua Tree*.

The plot thickens. The guys in U2, who are mainly Type Ones and Twos, became so upset that people like themselves were shunning them, they decided to break up. For a couple years around 1989-1990, U2 was defunct. Until they got the idea of reuniting and creating a new CD that would appeal strictly to people like themselves. *Achtung Baby* was the result (a decidedly One-ish sounding name, wouldn't you say?), and the music was so far left (on The influence Graph) that Type Ones adopted it immediately, declaring "U2 is back!"

Not everything moves all the way through The Influence Graph, however. Although *Achtung Baby* garnered Type One and Two acceptance, adoptive behavior dropped off there. Type Threes never did buy *Achtung Baby*, nor the next CD after that, the equally left-sided *Zooropa*, released in 1993.

Despite U2's triumphant comeback amongst Types One and Two, product sales were considerably lower than in the mass-appeal days (Types One and Two together are only 30 percent of the population). Mass media coverage, packed concert venues, and huge royalty checks do have a certain allure, especially after one has tasted that kind of success in the past. So in 1997, U2 reversed direction. They named their next CD *Pop* and began doing concerts at Kmart stores (I'm not kidding)! Kmart is right-sided Three and Four appeal. As lead singer Bono put it, "We need to be more mass appeal."

RESISTANCE BARRIERS

In the U2 example, we saw adoptive influence move through the entire Influence Graph, beginning with Type Ones and ending up with Type Fours. We also saw some adoptive behavior drop off and not move all the way through. Let's discuss this last point.

Sometimes a product or service has limited appeal and it does not move all the way through the population. *Resistance barriers* exist throughout The Influence Graph, and many products and services are affected by one or more. When susceptible products or services hit a resistance barrier, adoptive influence dwindles and people to the right of that point don't adopt.

The most pronounced line of demarcation is that which divides the Type Two and Three ranges. Remember, Types One and Two will put effort forth to acknowledge, understand, and appreciate that which is avant-garde, artsy, or subtle. Types Three and Four, however, don't put forth the effort to get into these things. Thus the adoptive influence of many avant-garde, artsy, or subtle things drops off rapidly as they hit the Type Three range.

You can see this happen quite often with certain movies, television shows, and CDs. For example, in early 1990 the television show "Twin Peaks" debuted on the ABC network and quickly became the buzz of the nation.* You couldn't live through 1990 without being exposed to media publicity and street talk about the show. With that kind of adoptive behavior on display, you'd expect influence to flow through The Influence Graph in no time, making the show one of the most watched shows in the country, wouldn't you? Yet "Twin Peaks" consistently languished in the bottom third of all network shows in the ratings. Why? The quirky show hit a resistance barrier between the Type Two and Three ranges, and adoption went no further. When you have a television show that garners only Type One and Two appeal, it will never generate high ratings.

Resistance barriers can appear anywhere, including in the middle of a Type range. The appeal of *GQ* magazine, for example, fades out in the middle of the Type Three range. U2's *Actung Baby* and *Zooropa* CDs faded in the middle of the Two range.

ADOPTIVE BEHAVIOR CAN BEGIN ANYWHERE

Please note that adoptive influence does not always begin at the very left side of The Influence Graph, with Type Ones. A behavior, the purchase of a product or service for example, can begin with any Influence Type. However, influence always moves from left to right, no matter where it begins.

J.C.Penney's appeal begins in the Two range and fades at the beginning of the Four range.

Maybelline cosmetics' appeal begins in the Three range, and extends through the Four range.

In the month of October each year, you can travel through some neighborhoods and see homes with huge orange pumpkin bags

---

*I'm using an example from many years ago so we have the benefit of tremendous hindsight. As you might expect with a show that never garnered Type Three or Four appeal, "Twin Peaks" never went into syndication after its initial network run. Which is why this may be the last time you ever hear of that show.

Plot it on The Influence Graph

Let's identify the appeal range of various products and services. Note that appeal ranges don't always start and end on the dividing line between Influence Types; they can start and end in the middle of the Types also.

Item	Appeal Range
Volkswagon Beetle	One, Two
Ford Taurus	Three, Four
Lincoln Continental	Three
Mercury Grand Marquis	Four
George Michael	One, Two, half of Three
Garth Brooks	Half of Three, Four
Madonna	One, Two, Three, Four
Absolut Vodka	One, Two, Three
Smirnoff Vodka	Three, Four
FedEx	One, Two, Three
UPS	Three, Four
U.S. Postal Service	Four
Levi's 501 jeans	One, half of Two
Levi's 505 jeans	Half of Two, Three
Levi's Slates	Two, Three
Levi's Dockers	Four
Apple Computer	One, Two, half of Three
Dell Computer	Half of Two, Three, Four
Gateway Computer	Half of Three, Four
Sharper Image	One, Two
Radio Shack	Three, Four
Christian Doir (cosmetics)	One, Two
Maybelline	Half of Three, Four
Bloomingdales	Half of One, Two, Half of Three
J.C. Penney	Half of Two, Three
Sears	Half of Three, Four
McCormick Crackers	Half of One, Two
Ritz Crackers	Three, Four

(which are leaf-gathering bags decorated like pumpkins) sitting on front lawns. This particular behavior began in the Four range and stays in the Four range.

PREDICT MARKETPLACE ACCEPTANCE OF A NEW PRODUCT OR SERVICE

Let's begin applying this material. We'll start with the simplest techniques and progress to the more complex.

Gauging acceptance of a new product or service before it's launched can save you a lot of time, money, and grief. Many marketers seem to rely on the trial-and-error method quite often, which is definitely the hard way. Others rely on test marketing, which does have its advantages at times. But a much easier method is available to you, utilizing the knowledge you now possess.

Simply determine how well your level of SAF newness matches your target Influence Type. By thinking about this ahead of time, you'll get a very reliable idea of how well your product or service will be accepted by what Influence Type.

You'll also get a good idea of the sales potential of your new product or service. Remember, Type Ones represent 10 percent of the population; Type Twos, 20 percent; Type Threes, 40 percent; Type Fours, 30 percent. You know even before you launch that if your product or service appeals to Ones and/or Twos, you're going to have a lot less sales than if it appeals to Threes and/or Fours. Remember also that adoptive influence moves from left to right through The Influence Graph, never from right to left. You may want initial Type One or Two acceptance, then grow sales over time as appeal moves into the Three and/or Four ranges. (Or you may want to keep sales in only one Influence Type over time. I'm not making any specific suggestion, I'm just pointing out the possibilities.)

GAIN QUICK MARKETPLACE ACCEPTANCE

Based on everything we've discussed in Chapter 15 and this chapter, you already know how to do this. You simply match your level of SAF newness (exuded by your product or service and its marketing) to the Influence Type you want to attract. You must design your advertising and media buys to make this match happen.

Let's say you wanted to open a new hotel that featured small rooms, no amenities, austere furniture, and aloof service. And you wanted to charge hundreds of dollars per night for a room. What Influence Type would you target to gain immediate marketplace acceptance?

Type Ones, of course. Which means the first thing you would do is make sure such a place had the right location. You'd pick cities with a large Type One population (or that attracts Type One visitors). In New York City, there's the Royalton and the Paramount. In Miami, the Delano Hotel; in San Francisco, the Diva Hotel (yes, these places really exist). Each fits the above description, and each claims upward of 90 percent occupancy at top-of-the-line room rates.

The quirkiness, stylishness, and uniqueness of these "boutique" hotels is classic Type One appeal. (Left-sided Type Twos might also be attracted.) If you can't believe that anyone would pay $200 to $400 a night for a tiny room with no amenities and rude service, you must be a Type Three or Four. Remember, there is no right or wrong, no good or bad associated with the various Influence Types. Just vastly different interests, and vastly different consumption behavior.

How would you advertise your new, chic hotel? Definitely not television — too mass appeal. Perhaps you'd use modern rock or alternative rock radio stations. And super-trendy local magazines would work. You get the idea.

GROW YOUR APPEAL WITH THE TARGET-LEFT STRATEGY

The *Target-Left Strategy* is a great way to begin spreading demand beyond the boundaries of one Influence Type. Here's how it works:

Determine which Influence Type you want to appeal to from a sales standpoint, then shift your marketing target to the left of this Type. The rule of thumb: Shift one-half an Influence Type to the left. For instance, if your sales target is primarily Type Threes, your marketing target will be the half-of-Two through half-of-Three range.

FIGURE 3
The Target-Left Strategy

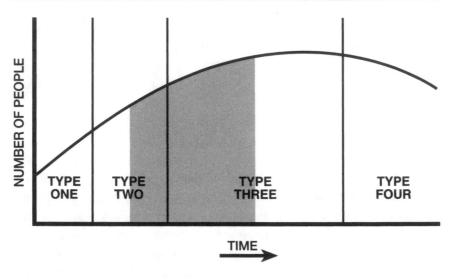

The shaded area is the optimum marketing target to affect Type Three individuals.

This is depicted in Figure 3.

By shifting your marketing target to the left of your sales target, two advantages occur.

First, you initiate adoption amongst hipper people than the ones you really want to purchase. In our example, right-sided Twos would begin adopting (having been persuaded to do so by your marketing targeted to them), and they would influence left-sided Threes to adopt through person-to-person human influence (in addition to any marketing reaching the left-sided Threes). Thus you would end up with stronger Type Three adoption than otherwise.

If, on the other hand, you did not shift your marketing target to the left and instead targeted the entire Three range head on, the people on the left side of the Three range wouldn't see the people to the left of them, the Twos, displaying any adoption. Adoptive human influence wouldn't be affecting the left-sided Threes. This would be unfortunate for you, since people — wherever they fall on The Influence Graph — are greatly influenced to do what the people slightly to the left of them are doing. And in this case, that wouldn't be happening.

Second, as you use the Target-Left Strategy, you widen your potential buying universe to include some people to the left of your actual sales target. Remember, influence travels only to the right, never to the left. If you target only Type Threes, Threes and Fours are all that you can potentially get. But when you include right-sided Twos in your target, you can potentially get half of Two, Three, and Four.

Examples of The Target-Left Strategy

Absolut is the number one selling brand of imported vodka in the United States. To sell as much as it does, it needs, and gets, acceptance throughout more than one Influence Type. Absolut's appeal range is Types One, Two, and Three. Yet Absolut targets its marketing to the left side of this range.

Here's another way of looking at it. Who influences the Threes to buy Absolut? Why, it's the Twos that do that. And who influences the Twos? The Ones do. By targeting their marketing to Types One and Two, and letting the natural flow of human influence take care of the Threes, they end up with One through Three acceptance.

Ralph Lauren's Polo brand of men's clothing also targets its marketing slightly to the left of its sales target. Polo's sales target is mainly Type Threes (women as well as men). It's marketing target is the half-of-Two through half-of-Three range (Figure 3, page 176).

Kmart and Wal-Mart both target right-sided Threes and Fours for sales. Yet their marketing is mainly targeted to the Three range. If you want Type Fours to purchase, you rarely have to market directly to them. By shifting your marketing to the left, adoptive influence steamrolls into the Four range on the impetus of previous adoption by Type Threes.

Implementation Example

Just how does a marketer shift their marketing to the left? Let's take Absolut as an example. Absolut targets Type Ones by exuding a very high level of SAF newness in *some* of its marketing. This starts with the package design. It has a very unusual-looking bottle, with an uncommonly short neck and no paper label. Absolut sponsors art exhibits around the country. Some of its ads employ lots of subtlety and artistry. It uses media outlets that have mainly Type One and some Two appeal for these high SAF newness ads, such as *Art & Antiques* and *Interview* magazines.

Absolut also prepares some ads with slightly less SAF newness and runs them in magazines with strong Type Two appeal (and which some Type Threes also read) such as *Rolling Stone, GQ,* and *Forbes.* Thus it has covered both ends of its One-to-Two marketing target (with some natural spillover into the Three range). This marketing target is about half an Influence Type to the left of its sales target.

WIDEN YOUR APPEAL BY ELIMINATING RESISTANCE BARRIERS

As I mentioned earlier, a resistance barrier can cause adoptive influence to stop moving through The Influence Graph. You needn't necessarily accept this. You can, in some cases, eliminate or reduce the effects of a resistance barrier, thereby allowing adoptive influence to continue moving through the population.

Resistance barriers exist for one reason: The level of SAF newness exuded by a product or service and its marketing is just too high for some people to accept, regardless of the adoptive influence they're exposed to. The way around this is to soften your level of SAF newness, in both your product or service and its marketing. That sounds simple, but it can be a major undertaking.

Incremental reductions in your SAF newness level tend to keep adoption moving through The Influence Graph. When a resistance barrier arises, however, it means major SAF adjustments, in both your product or service and its marketing, are required to eliminate the barrier and keep adoptive influence moving.

Which brings with it some potentially undesirable consequences. The major changes in your level of SAF newness required to eliminate the resistance barrier may have an adverse effect on the people you're already appealing to. If, for instance, your resistance barrier is located somewhere in the Type Three range, the lower level of SAF newness required to break through the barrier might repel Ones and Twos. Is that really what you want to happen?

In some cases, your answer may be yes. You may not care about driving away people to the left of your resistance barrier. The offsetting adoption by other people to the right of your resistance barrier may suit your wishes just fine. An example is Ford's Thunderbird. It was originally a Type Two-appeal car. Over the years, its appeal slowly moved to the right, eventually lodging in the Four range. For years, Thunderbird's marketing was Three-targeted (the Target-Left Strategy), and it's buyers were mainly Type Fours. (In the late '90s, Ford suspended production of the Thunderbird for a few years. Then they reintroduced it with a fresh '50s look, targeting Type Twos all over again.)

Be careful attempting to eliminate a resistance barrier. Sometimes you're better off with what you have than with what you might get. Absolut isn't interested in eliminating its resistance barrier, which falls on the line between the Types Three and Four ranges. To do so would require them to change practically their entire marketing approach, from the package to the advertising. It takes a wise marketer to realize the grass isn't always greener on the other side of the resistance barrier.

CREATE GARGANTUAN APPEAL THROUGH NEW-OLD BALANCE

Throughout this entire discussion of Influence Types, you may have been wondering if it's possible for a product or service to appeal to all four Types simultaneously. The answer is yes, it can be done. Examples include, but are not limited to, Pepsi, Madonna, the original *Batman* movie, Levi's, McDonald's, "Seinfeld" (the '90s TV show), and Coors Light. How do they keep Types One and Two from shunning while Types Three and Four adopt?

The secret to creating a *Gargantuan*, as it's called, is with *New-Old Balance*. To achieve a state of New-Old Balance, the marketer must provide an equal amount of SAF newness, which satisfies Types One and Two, and SAF sameness, which satisfies Types Three and Four. I must point out that this is very tricky. It can backfire if not done correctly. Let's see how some marketers are able to pull it off.

Coors Light

Ever notice that Coors Light has more than one ad campaign running at the same time? (If you didn't notice, it's probably because they run the different campaigns on different media outlets, reaching different Types with each.)

Some Coors Light television commercials feature Peter Coors standing in front of the Rockies talking about the pureness of the mountain water used to brew the beer. No music, no flashy graphics, no hype at all. This is Type One through half-of-Two appeal.

Another Coors Light campaign — running concurrently with the first — shows twenty-somethings bowling and throwing a frisbee in a surrealistic cloud-like surrounding. Half-of-Two through Three appeal.

Yet a third campaign — running concurrently with the other two — shows a guy wandering into a bar full of flannel-shirted male patrons. He starts singing "Rocky Mountain High," and the entire crowd joins in. Classic Type Four appeal.

Coors Light, with their various ad campaigns, has covered the entire Influence Graph. No wonder it sells so much beer to all kinds of different people.

McDonald's

McDonald's is a pillar of stability. You can walk into any McDonald's in the world and order a Big Mac, fries, and soft drink — the same items McDonald's has been selling for decades. A Big Mac from Detroit even looks and tastes the same as a Big Mac from Orlando, Los Angeles, Little Rock, or Tokyo. Each McDonald's store is clean, and each gives you good-tasting fast food. With McDonald's, you know what to expect. A high level of sameness is depicted in some of McDonald's ads and commercials. They even show Types Threes and Fours patronizing. That degree of aesthetic sameness and tradition is very attractive to Type Three and Four individuals.

But wait. While McDonald's is maintaining a stronghold on tradition, it's also changing. There's always a new promotion or contest going on. No two McDonald's stores are decorated alike. (One in New York has a grand piano in it. One in Richmond, Virginia, near the airport, has an airplane in it.) McDonald's experiments with different, adventurous, innovative architecture in its building designs. No single McDonald's ad or commercial runs for more than a few weeks; they're always changing. Some ads and commercials show Types One and Two patronizing, and are done in a very artsy style. The degree of SAF newness that McDonald's uses is just enough to keep the Ones and Twos feeling comfortable.

Madonna

If there's anyone who knows how to work The Influence Graph, it's Madonna. She does it through an exquisite display of New-Old Balance. Almost every one of her songs in a simple pop ditty that everyone from seven to 70 can tap their feet to, sing along with, and enjoy. Her music requires practically no effort to understand and appreciate. Madonna's music appears to have a low level of SAF newness, which appeals to Types Three and Four.

But wait. Every time another Madonna CD comes out, her appearance is completely different. Madonna's constantly changing her look, never staying with one look more than a year or so. And for those people who do put forth an effort when listening to her songs, many artistic nuances can be found. Lo and behold, the SAF newness is there after all. It just takes an effort to hear it. Her videos are on the cutting edge of artistic innovation. In fact, she often pushes the edge to its extreme. Madonna shows enough SAF newness for Types One and Two to justify their acceptance and override any shunning tendencies.

"Seinfeld"

The "Seinfeld" television show has (I'll use the present tense, even though the show is no longer in production. You will, after all, continue to see it for years in syndication) four main characters. Which is the Type One? Kramer. Which is the Type Two? Elaine. The Type Three? Jerry. And the Type Four? George. (You can tell which Type they are simply by their dress.) One character for each Influence Type. No wonder the show was a ratings winner for so long.

A couple interesting asides. The Kramer character is a middle-aged Type One, who dresses in clothes from the '50s (what's old is new). An example, admittedly exaggerated, of how an older Type One might dress differently than a younger Type One.

Here's a question for you: Would Kramer, a Type One, and George, a Type Four, ever hang out together if they didn't have a mutual friend, Jerry, in the middle? Not likely. Type Ones and Type Fours live in different, non-intersecting worlds, for the most part. Even on the show you only see Kramer and George together when they're with Jerry.

Your Turn

You can employ New-Old Balance as well. It's a matter of keeping some aspects of your product or service and its marketing the same year after year, thus exuding a low level of SAF newness, and constantly displaying new style, art, and fashion aspects, thus exuding a high level of SAF newness.

You don't have to be a large-scale marketer with deep pockets to utilize New-Old Balance. Pleasants Hardware is a small home improvement company in Richmond, Virginia. They play up the fact that they've been in existence for over 75 years. Their advertising emphasizes the fact that Pleasants is "a time-honored tradition." And they carry the same old tools and fix-up items you'd expect in any hardware store. Three and Four appeal.

Yet its slogan is "The Great Big Toy Store for Adults," a somewhat off-the-wall slogan for a hardware store. The exterior of their main store, located inside the city limits, has a unique design that is updated periodically. The interior features classy burgundy carpeting, low ceilings with exposed air ducts painted cobalt blue, and adventurous lighting arrangements. They also carry trendy decorative items that change all the time. Remember, this is a hardware store, inherently SAF-light. But by boosting its level of SAF newness just enough, Type One and Two appeal results. It's also interesting to note that Pleasants' other location, at the outskirts of suburbia, exudes a much lower lever of SAF newness. All together, the New-Old Balance attracts people of all four Influence Types.

I said earlier that New-Old Balance is tricky. The danger lies in confusing people, of seeming to be one thing sometimes and something else at other times. A blurred image, so to speak. I wish I could give you a one-sentence, definitive answer to help you out here. The truth is, however, marketers who use New-Old Balance effectively rely on their supreme instinct and intuitive wisdom to pull it off. If you don't have the "feel" for it, it may be best not to attempt it. Instead, try the next strategy, which is much easier to implement.

HEDGE YOUR BET WITH THE STRADDLE STRATEGY

Let's say you don't have the financial resources to have multiple ad campaigns running concurrently. And you don't have the instincts to attempt New-Old Balance. You may still be able to appeal to most of The Influence Graph using the relatively simple *Straddle Strategy.* (The Straddle Strategy is not as powerful as New-Old Balance, and cannot produce the same Gargantuan results. It is more economical and less risky, however.)

Design your product or service and its marketing such that the level of SAF newness you're exuding is smack dab in the middle of The Influence Graph. In other words, you straddle the line between the Type Two and Type Three ranges.

Here's why this position tends to be the most powerful position on the board. Type Ones are disenfranchised, for the most part. They go through life realizing that very few things are targeted to people like themselves. So if a product or service even leans in their direction, exuding some Type Two appeal let's say, Type Ones adoptively accept it quite often. In other words, unless your product or service is specifically designed for Type Ones, you really don't have to appeal to Type Ones directly to gain their patronage (albeit non-evangelistic patronage).

And unless your product or service is designed specifically for Type Fours, you don't have to target them directly either. Adoptive influence from the Type Threes will take care of the Type Fours automatically (assuming there's no resistance barrier there in your case).

So you really only need to direct your marketing to Twos and Threes to appeal to most of The Influence Graph.

With the Straddle Strategy, all you have to do is alter one or two minor style, art, and fashion elements and your appeal leans in either the One/Two direction or the Three/Four direction.

I do this with my appearance. Ninety percent of my appearance plots me right on the straddle line between the Type Two and Type Three ranges. Then, all I need do is alter one or two elements of my appearance — my glasses or tie, for example — and I appear to be a Type Two or a Type Three. Depending on who I want to appeal to (or my mood that day), I lean one way or the other.*

You can do this with your marketing materials or logo. Straddle the Two/Three line with most of it, then alter one or two elements to lean it whichever way you choose. For example, you might mail your brochure in a conservative white or gray envelope to Type Threes or Fours, or in a fluorescent lavender envelope to Type Ones or Twos. When you straddle, and alter one small aspect of your SAF newness level, you may match different Influence Types without it costing you a bundle.

INSTIGATE SHUNNING THROUGH NEGATIVE INFLUENCE

As I've mentioned before, shunning occurs when people are influenced to stop a particular behavior or not to engage in it in the first place. In most cases, shunning is not something a marketer strives for, at least not for his own product or service.

But there are a couple instances in which you might want to instigate shunning. For one, you may wish to cause people to shun a competing product or service. For another, you may wish to cause a socially, morally, legally, or otherwise undesirable behavior, such as drug abuse or shoplifting, to subside.

Shunning is caused by *negative influence.* Up to this point, when I spoke of human influence, I was referring to positive human influence. That is, influence that persuades a person to adopt some type of behavior. Negative influence, on the other hand, persuades a person to stop a certain behavior or never to begin adoption. You saw

---

*I'm a left-sided Type Three. I can lean in either the Two or Three direction and feel comfortable. I'm not suggesting any of us try to become an Influence Type we're not comfortable being.

evidence of negative influence earlier when we discovered that Type Ones tend to shun certain products or services when they see Types Three and Four adopting.

How Negative Influence Works

People are positively influenced by people slightly to the left of themselves on The Influence Graph, that is, by people similar to themselves though slightly more receptive to SAF newness. People are negatively influenced by others who are unlike themselves, that is, by people who are one-and-a-half to two Influence Types away from them (in either direction). In that sense, what is positive influence to some can be negative influence to others at the same time.

I emphasized earlier that there are no good or bad values attached to the various Influence Types. It's no better to be any particular Type than it is to be any other Type. We all know people of all Influence Types, and we can love and respect them all. As a marketer, you must maintain this unbiased perspective to utilize this concept to your advantage.

But people out there in the marketplace do have biases toward one another. The Type Ones, for instance, view the Type Fours as "square," "unhip," or "out of it." When they see the Type Fours adopting something, that influences the Type Ones to shun that particular behavior. Thus the Type One has been negatively influenced.

The Type Fours view the Type Ones as "kooks," or "wierdos," who have "no touch with reality." When a Four sees a One adopting a particular product or service, the Four determines it's not for her. She has been negatively influenced.

Although less intense than the bias that exists between the polarized Ones and Fours, bias exists between other Influence Types as well. And no matter where any of us falls on The Influence Graph, we think we're "normal" and others farther away from us are "abnormal." Like George Carlin's bit about driving along the highway. If someone is driving faster than us he's a maniac, and if someone is driving slower than us he's an idiot. Wherever we are, we're "correct."

Inadvertent Influence

A marketer could inadvertently nurture negative influence by using the wrong type of people in its advertising. When Levi's introduced their Dockers line of men's slacks years ago, they showed Type Four males wearing them. As you would expect, Type Fours bought and wore them. Also as you might expect, Types One and Two, and most Type Threes, shunned them. After a few years, Dockers sales stopped growing. Which prompted Levi's to revamp their advertising utilizing hipper-looking models. It worked somewhat, in that adoptive behavior amongst Type Threes increased a little. But once a product or service is strongly branded as "belonging" to a particular Influence Type, it's very difficult to change that image. Levi's simply resigned itself to market Dockers as a Type Four-appeal product, and they created a whole new brand of slacks, called Slates, to appeal to Type Threes.

A more common mistake is when a company's marketing is too far left and their product or service never gains the mass appeal they desire. This happens when the creative people in ad agencies, who are almost exclusively Type Ones and Twos, fail to understand that they should be creating advertising that appeals to people unlike themselves. When working with an ad agency, the onus falls on you to discuss this with them and keep them from producing ads that are not targeting the Influence Type(s) you desire.

Shunning Procedures

Here are the steps to use if you want to instigate shunning:
- **Step 1: Determine what Influence Type you want to shun.** Let's say you want Type Twos to shun a competing soft drink, for example.
- **Step 2: Depict adoption by a non-adjacent Influence Type.** The non-adjacent Influence Type to a Two is a Four (Types One and Three are adjacent to Type Two on The Influence Graph.) Create an ad or commercial showing Fours adopting the competing drink.

    This is exactly what Pepsi did. In a television commercial, they showed singer M.C. Hammer in concert singing one of his songs. M.C. Hammer's appeal was in the half-of-Two through Three range at the time. Well, someone switches his soft drink from Pepsi to Coke, and after inadvertently taking a swig of Coke, he suddenly bursts into "Feelings," an old Morris Albert hit from 1975, and a quintessential Four-appeal song. People in the audience can't figure out what's happened to M.C. until someone offers him a Pepsi, and after drinking it he shifts back into his normal song. The message, directed to Twos and Threes: Coke is for "un-hip" people and Pepsi is for "hip" people like you.

   Note: You needn't necessarily mention competing brands by name to instigate shunning (in fact, you enter dangerous legal territory if you do so). References to types of products or services in a more general fashion can be just as effective.

- **Step 3: Use media outlets or programs that appeal to the Type you want to shun.** You may not want everyone and anyone to be aware of your shun-instigating ads or commercials. Think what would happen if Type Fours saw Pepsi's M.C. Hammer commercial. They probably wouldn't get the point, since the song "Feelings" wouldn't be a turn-off to them. The message they would get is that Pepsi is for people unlike themselves, and Coke is for them. This Pepsi commercial would actually strengthen Coke's appeal among Fours, not something Pepsi wants to happen (Pepsi wants to remain a Gargantuan, with universal appeal). That's why Pepsi only ran this particular commercial in television programs whose appeal did not extend into the Four range.

Chapter Seventeen

The Inattentive State: How People Receive Advertising

The question is not whether or not the public pays attention to advertising. We all know there is a serious lack of attention to ads and commercials. The real question is: What can you, the marketer, do to overcome the condition?

I've run into very few marketers who know how to deal properly with the lack of attention their ads and commercials naturally engender. Although in every ad campaign strategy session there's always someone who stands up and excitedly declares, "But first we've got to get their attention!", I can assure you that "attention getting" is not the optimum solution to the problem. In truth, your advertising must be effective whether people are paying attention or not, and I'm going to show you how to make that happen.

In the next two chapters you will learn specific strategies and techniques to improve your advertising effectiveness tremendously in our attention-poor environment. But first we must step back and look at *how* people behave at the receiving end of advertising, and *why* so many people aren't paying attention in the first place.

THE ATTENTION DILEMMA

Let's say you have a television commercial currently running on a few stations or networks and a print ad running in a newspaper. How important is it to you that people pay attention to your commercial and ad? Does the effectiveness of your commercial and ad depend on whether or not people are paying attention to it? Most marketers feel the effectiveness of their advertising depends a great deal on the amount of attention it can garner. After all, if you don't have peoples' attention, you may as well be talking to the wall, right?

Your dilemma is, however, that only a small percentage of the people watching television any time your commercial airs, or flipping past your newspaper ad, will actually pay attention to it. (Lack of attention to advertising occurs in all media outlet types, not just television and newspaper. However, to keep our discussion from getting too unwieldy, I'll stick mainly with these two for now.) That's easy to understand. It's obvious that television viewers tune in to watch the programming content, not the commercial content. Likewise, the newspaper reader seeks news, not advertisements.

It's interesting to observe people as they watch television or read a newspaper. Here's an experiment I'd like you to try. Watch what television viewers do when a commercial comes on. Chances are, they will turn their attention elsewhere. They actually turn their heads away from the television and toward something or someone else in the room. They'll engage in some other activity, such as picking up some reading material, letting out the dog, conversing with someone, looking out the window, or visiting the bathroom or kitchen.*

Next time you're watching a television program with other people in the room, see how long it takes for someone to begin speaking when a commercial comes on. People have been conditioned to con-

---

*A Roper poll, published in *TV Guide* in the mid 1990s, revealed these results: While watching television, one-half of all adults get up to do something else during commercials, fewer than one in four stay in their seats, one-third talk to others in the room, one-quarter switch channels, and one in seven turn the sound down.

verse with one another during commercials. It never fails. I will bet you someone in the room will begin speaking within five seconds from when the first commercial begins, every time. ("Zapping," or "channel surfing," when viewers grab the remote and change the channel during a commercial break, is another matter altogether. This discussion deals with people who are at least exposed to a commercial, yet do not pay attention to it.)

TWENTY PERCENT IS (GENEROUSLY) ALL YOU GET

Just what percentage of people who are exposed to the average ad or commercial pay conscious attention to it? That is a difficult question to answer. If we piece together various research studies, including one conducted by my own firm, we can conclude that roughly 20 percent — one person out of five — is consciously paying attention to the average ad or commercial each time they're exposed to it. That means 80 percent of the people are not paying conscious attention to an ad or commercial each time they're exposed to it.

Does that surprise you? Most industry professionals in advertising and marketing that I've mentioned this 20 percent figure to are surprised it's that high. Most guess the attention level would be closer to 10 percent. Seems my 20 percent estimate is very generous. (Don't get bogged down debating the numbers. A highly accurate, scientifically valid figure is probably impossible to obtain and isn't really necessary. A 20 percent attention level is in the ballpark, and is a good working number for our purposes.)

INTRODUCTION TO INATTENTION

Most of the time people simply do not pay conscious attention to advertising. Not because so many ads and commercials are boring or irrelevant; they're not. Not because so many ads and commercials are poorly produced; they're not. But because people are predisposed to divert their attention elsewhere, regardless of all those other factors. With regard to advertising, *people don't want to pay attention*. It's as simple as that.

We call the lack of attention *inattention*. When the brain drops into a state of inattention with regard to the matter in question, that person is said to be in an *inattentive state*.

Have you ever driven past the highway exit you intended to use? With regard to your driving, you were in an inattentive state. At the same time, you were probably in an *attentive state* with regard to something else . . . talking to a passenger or thinking about a problem, perhaps. Have you ever found yourself mentally "tuning out" while your spouse or child was speaking to you? With regard to the other person's speaking, your brain was in an inattentive state, although you may have been in an attentive state with regard to something else at the time.

WHY INATTENTION OCCURS

People have learned to go into a state of inattention when an ad or commercial reaches their brain. There are three main reasons why this programmed inattention happens.

- **Reason 1: People have been conditioned to treat a commercial as a "break" or "interruption" in the programming.** Ever since the advent of radio and television, broadcasters have used phrases like, "Now a word from our sponsor," "We'll be back after this," or "When we return . . . " which tell the viewer or listener to divert his attention. Once conditioned, the viewer needn't even hear those words to go into the inattentive state. The appearance of the first commercial in the break will often trigger the state.

  With newspapers and magazines, the inattentive state with respect to ads is programmed into the reader's mind for exactly the opposite reason. Most newspapers and magazines intentionally ignore the fact that they have ads in them. By doing so they condition the reader to ignore the ads as well.

  Say you're reading an article on page D1 and at the bottom of the page it says, "Continued on page D17." So you flip to D17 and continue reading. The fact that there were 16 pages in between D1 and D17, containing numerous ads, was never mentioned. Should the newspaper have said, "Please read the ads on pages D2 through D16 before going to the remainder of this article on page D17"?

Before you blame the media for causing inattention, realize that no other alternative is really feasible. The distinct separation of program and/or editorial content and commercial content is desirable for reasons other than those of interest to the marketer. It goes back to some of the principles upon which this country was founded, including the freedom of speech and independence of thought. Newspapers and news broadcasts (collectively referred to as "the press") would not be able to maintain journalistic integrity if they bowed to commercial interests.

That's not to say some marketers haven't devised ways of blurring the lines anyway. Have you ever seen a newspaper ad that looked just like a news story in wording and design? The newspaper requires that the word "Advertisement" appear at the top of the ad to distinguish it, but the marketer is hoping you don't notice that word.

Then there are infomercials . . . program-length television commercials in the guise of an actual program.

And perhaps the ultimate in commercial-program blending occurs when marketers pay movie studios to have their product or service show up in a scene or two. Come to think of it, I just saw James Bond talking on an Ericsson phone, drinking Smirnoff vodka, watching a Sony television, smashing a souped-up BMW, and returning it to Avis. (Good to know he lives in the real world.)

- **Reason 2: Inattention exists because of a mental function called** *state default.* Inattention is a relaxed state which normally dominates unless it is overridden by a more powerful stimulus. In the absence of overriding stimuli, the brain defaults into the inattentive state. Since advertising is not important to most people, their brains assign it a very low value. A value that usually is not strong enough to switch the mind into an attentive state when exposed to an ad or commercial.
- **Reason 3: People consciously plan to divert their attention in the first place.** Have you ever had the television or radio on even though you were consciously paying attention to some-

thing else . . . cleaning the house, playing cards, working, or eating perhaps? "Wallpaper video," when the television is on but no one is really watching, is commonplace. And radio has been used as "background" for years. Sometimes we "read" the newspaper by flipping through the pages in rapid succession, stopping only to absorb a headline or two along the way. In these cases, the viewer, listener, or reader is in the inattentive state with regard to the entire thing — program/editorial content and commercial content combined.

HOW DO YOU HANDLE INATTENTION?

So, what are we going to do about the inattentive state? Here are the three most popular strategies — none of which I recommend. (After we review these three, we'll be ready to discuss the real answer.)

The Ostrich Strategy

As incredible as it may seem, many marketers do nothing about the fact that the majority of the people they're paying to reach through the media are not paying attention to their advertising. Even when they acknowledge the lack of attention, they usually ignore it. And some marketers want to believe that people are paying attention to their ads and commercials, mentally denying all the logical evidence to the contrary.

Ad agencies and media outlets tend to reinforce this false belief. Understandable when you realize that to do otherwise — to acknowledge any weakness in the system — might be committing professional suicide. What agency, after all, will tell a client it's just produced a wonderful television commercial that most people are not going to pay attention to? That's the last thing you'd want to bring up when you're trying to impress a client with your incredible talent and expertise. And what media outlet would dare point out that all those viewers or readers it boasts are paying attention to the programming or editorial content but not the advertising?

Consequently, some marketers function as though everything they do will have a major impact — that people will hang on every word and respond in droves. These marketers are always the ones who suffer from chronic disappointment and frustration with the ensuing results. Yet they plod on.

The Bang-Away Strategy

If only one person out of five is paying conscious attention to an ad or commercial each time it runs, why not run the ad or commercial five times and thereby catch everyone in the attentive state at least once? There's no reason why not. The practice of using multiple exposures, or frequency, is an integral part of advertising. The concept is as old as advertising itself. In fact, if you're not running your ads or commercials with healthy frequency, chances are you're falling short of the results threshold.

I'll assume that you, as the no-wet-behind-the-ears marketer that you are, are already running your ads and commercials with good frequency. How do you increase their effectiveness even further? Do you simply increase the frequency even further?

Yes, higher frequency equals higher effectiveness . . . to a point. But diminishing returns set in before long, beyond which additional exposures produce little if any additional result.* Yet some marketers behave as though effectiveness keeps increasing the more they bang away.

Most marketers who implement the *Bang-Away Strategy* at one time or another eventually give up on it. One can only spend so much money before lack of acceptable return forces one to back off.

The Clutter Buster Strategy

In the 1980s, the *Clutter Buster Strategy* developed. The idea is to attract attention by having your ad or commercial jump out from all the others which surround it. In television, for example, your commercial must somehow "bust through the clutter" to be noticed, the "clutter" being all the other commercials on the air. In other words,

---

*For a definitive and highly technical explanation, read *Effective Frequency: The Relationship Between Frequency and Advertising Effectiveness* by Michael J. Naples (Association of National Advertisers, Inc., 1979.)

every advertiser considers every other advertiser's commercials as part of the clutter. In the eyes of other advertisers, your commercial is the clutter they're trying to bust out of. How do you like that?

The Clutter Buster Strategy has resulted in an improvement in the overall quality of commercials and ads, no doubt. But since every marketer is trying to break through the clutter of every other marketer's ads and commercials, the net result is close to zero. Like all the runners in a pack deciding to pour on a burst of speed at once to break out, the entire pack moves faster, but it's still a pack.

Truly, a high quality ad or commercial is essential these days to keep from dropping back of the pack rather than to bust out of it.

THE REAL ANSWER TO GREATER AD EFFECTIVENESS

If the Ostrich Strategy, Bang-Away Strategy, and Clutter Buster Strategy all come up short, what is the answer to the inattentive state? How to we increase the effectiveness of our advertising in this attention-deprived world?

Would you believe the answer lies in *not* increasing the level of attention of your ads or commercials above what they naturally garner? If you think I'm kidding, consider this: *People do not want your ad or commercial to kick them into attention.* They're perfectly happy being in the inattentive state when they see or hear your ad or commercial. In fact, all people, you and I included, have an instinctive defence mechanism in place to keep the majority of ads and commercials from getting our conscious attention.

Therefore, if you're trying to constantly get people's attention, you're fighting the natural desires of the consumer. It's like a tug of war you've got going. You're pulling in one direction, the consumer is pulling in the other. And you're going to lose that war 99 percent of the time no matter what you do.

One of the tenets upon which this book is based is that the marketer can achieve the highest levels of success only by catering to the inmost needs and desires of the consumer. Fighting the consumer is not the answer to creating demand. The real answer to incredible advertising impact, in which the marketer and consumer work together, will be revealed in the next chapter. Meet you there.

Chapter Eighteen

The Simulconscious Strategy

Here's the good news you've been waiting for: It doesn't matter whether people are paying attention to your advertising or not. You can increase the effectiveness of your advertising significantly even when the majority of people that are exposed to it are in the inattentive state. The idea is to program your commercial or ad for people in the inattentive state as well as for those in the attentive state. It's called the *Simulconscious Strategy*. The process itself is called *simulconsciousing*.

When you implement the Simulconscious Strategy, you actually design your ad or commercial to penetrate and impress the conscious mind (which takes care of those who are paying conscious attention to it), and the subconscious mind (which affects those not paying any attention to it). And you do both simultaneously.

HOW SIMULCONSCIOUSING WORKS

Preparing your message for people in the attentive state is easy. That's what you're already doing. Preparing your commercial for people in the inattentive state is not any more difficult, but it is different. It may even seem a bit awkward at first.

When you program your ad or commercial for inattentive reception, you're introducing certain elements which penetrate the subconscious mind and make subconscious impressions. Affecting the subconscious mind is vitally important because (*a*) most often it is the subconscious mind that controls want and desire (remember, the power-wants are deeply subconscious), and (*b*) subconscious impressions affect memory and top-of-mind-awareness, both important factors in demand creation.

Here's the real beauty of it: People in the inattentive state are only inattentive on the conscious level. Their subconscious minds remain wide open for impression in the inattentive state.

When you are simulconsciousing, you prepare your ad or commercial in such a manner as to penetrate and impress the subconscious mind as well as the conscious mind. Therefore, an impression is made regardless of which state — attentive or inattentive — a person is in at the time of exposure.

HOW A SIMULCONSCIOUS COMMERCIAL IS RECEIVED

Consider what happens at the receiving end of a television commercial, starting with a regular, non-simulconsciously constructed commercial.

An attentive viewer will consciously see whatever appears on the screen and hear whatever is contained on the audio track. I'm not saying such a person is scrutinizing the commercial and detecting every detail. I'm saying an attentive viewer is paying just enough attention to be consciously aware of the commercial and get the gist of the message.

With the inattentive viewer it's another story. Although the inattentive viewer's eyes may cross the television screen for a portion of the time the commercial is on, and the audio may enter the viewer's ears, the message *doesn't make an impression*. The viewer is simply not paying attention; his or her conscious mind is on something else at the moment. *For the inattentive viewer, the commercial didn't even exist* (except to provide break time for a kitchen run or to talk to someone in the room, perhaps). And remember, at least 80 percent of the viewers at any given time are in the inattentive state.

Why didn't our commercial make an impression on the inattentive viewer? Because the commercial was not constructed with the purpose of penetrating the subconscious mind. It was constructed under the assumption that people will pay conscious attention to it. (Or as happens most of the time, it was constructed to pass the muster of paying clients and ad execs who are actually scrutinizing it.)

Now look what happens in the case of a simulconsciously constructed commercial.

For the attentive viewer, the commercial appears no different from the non-simulconsciously constructed commercial. That is, the differences wouldn't likely be detected by the untrained observer. The attentive viewer, you'll recall, is not scrutinizing the commercial, only paying nominal attention.

The inattentive viewer, on the other hand, is not aware of the commercial on the conscious level, which is no different from what occurs with the non-simulconscious version. But here's where things begin to differ greatly. As the inattentive viewer's eyes cross the television screen once or twice and his or her ears receive the audio portion, *certain material from both the video and audio penetrate their subconscious mind and make valuable impressions.* Why does this happen? Because the commercial was specially constructed to be received on the subconscious level, that's why. Which is what the Simulconscious Strategy is all about. You program your ads and commercials with specific information that registers consciously and subconsciously. This will become even clearer as you read the remainder of this chapter and the next.

NOT SUBLIMINAL PERCEPTION

Do not confuse simulconsciousing with subliminal perception. The two are completely different, in this way:

When you program a message for subliminal perception, you specifically design it to bypass the conscious mind entirely and go straight to the subconscious. For example, perhaps you've heard one of those subliminal self-improvement tapes which everyone and his uncle is marketing these days. All you consciously hear is music or ocean waves. The actual behavior-influencing message is at an inaudible level and can be detected only by your subconscious mind. The message has been prepared for perception by the subconscious mind only.

With the Simulconscious Strategy, you do not attempt to bypass the conscious mind at all. There are no "subliminal messages" which the receiver cannot consciously detect. Unlike messages designed for subliminal perception, which pre-determines they will be received strictly on the subconscious level, simulconsciousing does not pre-determine at which level of consciousness they will be received. Rather, each person receiving the message determines how he or she will receive the message — consciously or subconsciously — based on whether he or she is in the attentive or inattentive state at the time.

What Song Are You Singing Right Now?

Have you ever caught yourself humming or singing a particular song, either in your mind or out loud, at a time when you were not actually hearing the song? You probably heard the song on the radio or somewhere else hours or days earlier, but you don't remember hearing it. You were in the inattentive state at the time you heard the song, yet it made an impression on your subconscious mind nonetheless, and now you're humming it some time later.

The song was not some subliminal piece of information. *It was perfectly audible on the conscious level, even though you weren't listening to it on the conscious level.*

Ever catch yourself singing a commercial jingle? Same thing happened. Or how about verbally repeating something you heard or read some time before? You can't remember where you heard or saw it, but here you are talking about it.

Are you starting to see how powerful simulconsciousing is, how it can really propel the effectiveness of your advertising?

THE SIMULCONSCIOUS AD ELEMENTS

As you'll recall from our discussion of pre-processing in Chapter 10, only certain pieces of information are likely to penetrate the subconscious mind and make an instant impression. All the other stuff — the vast amount of information the subconscious mind receives but cannot handle without sending it to the conscious mind for processing — makes no impact most of the time.

There are three pieces of information which are powerful enough to make subconscious impressions on people in the inattentive state. We call them the *simulconscious ad elements*. When you are simulconsciousing, you include the simulconscious ad elements in your ad or commercial in a specific manner.

The Simulconscious Ad Elements:

- Your pre-processed word.
- Your logo or brand name.
- Your point line.

The first simulconscious ad element is your pre-processed word. The second is your logo or brand name. Both of these were discussed in Chapter 10. The third element is your *point line,* which we'll discuss now.

A point line is a one-sentence explanation or summary of what you're trying to get across in your ad or commercial. It is, simply, the point.

How do you create a point line? Imagine someone who is exposed to your ad or commercial, someone who has neither the time nor interest in your commercial to give it any conscious attention, shouting to you, "What are you trying to tell me here? I don't have the time or energy to devote to your commercial, so just give me the point in as few words as possible!" Your answer, delivered as succinctly as possible, is your point line. (You may want to spend some time honing and revising it, of course, as part of the creation process.)

A point line is not necessarily the same thing as a slogan, although the two can be one and the same in certain instances. Slogans most often make a point about a company as opposed to a specific product. They also tend to be image-oriented, rather than about a specific offer. A point line, on the other hand, summarizes the specific message in the ad or commercial in which it appears. The point line may vary from ad to ad, whereas a slogan may remain the same and transcend any one ad campaign.

State Farm has some ads and commercials with a point line that says, "State Farm sells life insurance." Perfect! That point line, straight and simple, will make a much stronger impression than anything else in the commercial, excluding perhaps the pre-processed word or logo (which are the other two simulconscious ad elements).

Your point line is the essence of a particular ad or commercial. It's what you want to get across, what you want them to remember.

THE RESULTS OF SIMULCONSCIOUSING

Of those in the inattentive state who receive exposure to your advertising, the simulconscious ad elements are all that will penetrate their minds. And sometimes not all three elements will make it. Although your pre-processed word and logo or brand name make an impression virtually 100 percent of the time a person sees or hears them, your point line will make an impression only about half the time.

What little, insignificant impression you may think you are making actually has a cumulative effect that builds up over time. As subconscious impressions build, they begin to shape the way a person thinks and acts. Results, in one word. That's why it's important to program your ads for the subconscious mind was well as the conscious mind at all times.

The results you achieve from implementing the Simulconscious Strategy can be dramatic. Rising notoriety, rising sales. And they can begin to happen soon after implementation!

EXACTLY HOW DO YOU DO SIMULCONSCIOUSING?

How you integrate the simulconscious ad elements into your ads and commercials is critical. The form in which the three simulconscious ad elements appear is as important as the elements themselves.

Because the optimum form varies depending on medium, we'll discuss precisely how to construct your advertising using the Simulconscious Strategy for specific mediums in the next chapter.

Chapter Nineteen

How to Double the Effectiveness of Your Advertising at No Additional Cost

Okay, you've flipped ahead to this chapter to find out what in the world could possibly double your advertising's effectiveness at no cost. I won't keep you waiting. The secret is to use the Simulconscious Strategy. It's the integration of the simulconscious ad elements — your pre-processed word, logo or brand name, and point line — into your ads and commercials in a very specific manner.

Readers who have reached this chapter by way of the previous 18 chapters are entitled to smirk. They know you have no idea what I'm talking about. You see, this whole demand creation business, including the doubling of your advertising's effectiveness, is a building process. Each successive move you make builds upon your previous moves. In other words, you've got to read and implement what I've presented in the preceding 18 chapters before you'll be ready to do any effectiveness doubling. This chapter will still be here when you get back.

For those who are ready, let's begin.

When your ad or commercial is properly simulconscioused, it affects people who are paying attention to it — those in the attentive state — and it affects people who are not paying attention to it — those in the inattentive state. Compared to a non-simulconscioused ad or commercial, which affects only those in the attentive state, your simulconscioused ad or commercial is twice as effective.

Actually, the effectiveness of your advertising may more than double. Since 80 percent of the receivers of each ad or commercial are in the inattentive state, you really have the potential of tripling, quadrupling, or quintupling your effectiveness when you start affecting these people. But let's be very conservative and say we have a high degree of confidence that the effectiveness of our advertising will at least double when we are simulconsciousing.

As for the costs, that stays the same. It costs you no more to simulconscious your ads or commercials, from either a production or media buying standpoint.

One more thing before we begin. As is the case with every strategy and technique in this book, simulconsciousing works for both the small-scale marketer and the large-scale marketer. Whether you're a one-person entrepreneur with a smallish ad budget, or one of the world's top advertisers, simulconsciousing will work for you. I point this out to keep you from getting the impression simulconsciousing is meant for marketers unlike yourself. It's for you.

HOW TO SIMULCONSCIOUS YOUR TELEVISION COMMERCIALS

Simulconsciously constructing your television commercials does not mean you must alter the concept, theme, or storyline from what they would otherwise be. Integrating the simulconscious ad elements into your commercials won't displace any other elements in the commercials. For the most part, things remain intact.

However, incorporating your simulconscious ad elements will alter the "look and feel" of the commercial somewhat. Its style and format will be affected. This is a good thing, since such affection will boost your commercial's effectiveness . . . which is why you're advertising in the first place, right?

Here is the specific procedure to simulconscious your television commercials:

- **Step 1: Begin your commercial with your pre-processed word and logo.** Your pre-processed word and logo should appear at the same time. They should be on the screen the first 1 to 1.5 seconds of your commercial.

    Here's an example. In a McDonald's McRib commercial, the McDonald's logo appeared for the first second or two in the lower right hand corner of the screen, superimposed over the scene of a family looking hungry and excited. Then the word "Hungry?" was superimposed over the action scene.(It would have been even better to show the word "Hungry?" and the logo in that sequential order, or both at the same time, rather than the logo first and then the pre-processed word. But this is a decent example, nonetheless.)

    Your pre-processed word and logo needn't be the only two things on the screen for the first 1.5 seconds. They can be superimposed over the action, as in this McDonald's commercial.

    One of the biggest mistakes marketers make is to wait until the end of their commercial to show their logo, as though they feel compelled to make some sort of statement first, then finally reveal it's them making the statement. That would be like someone calling you on the phone and talking for 30 or 60 seconds before telling you who is calling. Very annoying, wouldn't you say? And that's why identifying yourself right off the bat is what we all do when placing a phone call to someone. So why would you want to hold back your identity when communicating with people via a television commercial? Are you afraid people will tune out if they realize it's you?

    The first 1.5 seconds of a television commercial is when the viewer's brain is most receptive to influence, even in the inattentive state. It's the most important part of your commercial, which is why your logo needs to be on the screen then. In the first 1.5 seconds, the viewers defenses are at their lowest point. It's when the brain actually welcomes information instead of blocking it out. In fact, the brain uses the information it receives in the first 1.5

seconds to decide what state to assume, attentive or inattentive. Your logo makes its strongest possible impact during this brief window of welcome.

Hey! If this is true, if the viewer uses the first 1.5 seconds to help determine his state, why not present something that jolts the viewer into attention? There are two reasons why not. First, people have seen it all so many times before, they've become numb to whatever "jolting" information you might present. (The only surefire attention-triggers left are the words "News Bulletin" or "Breaking News," or a naked person, neither of which you can likely use.)

Second, as I mentioned before, you're fighting the viewer when your main objective is to jolt her to attention. The viewer doesn't want to pay attention most of the time. What the viewer does want at the beginning of a commercial is an answer to the question, "Who is about to speak to me?" Give him the answer he instinctively seeks, and you will have a better chance to keep him around for whatever else you have to say.

- **Step 2: Show your logo repeatedly throughout your commercial.** Even in the inattentive state, a viewer's eyes cross the screen periodically (if they remain in the room). Although the brain is less receptive to information throughout a commercial than in the first 1.5 seconds, the brain will still register information it doesn't have to process.

  You don't know when an inattentive viewer's eyes happen to be on the screen. They may see only a few seconds of your commercial . . . at the beginning or various other places as their eyes roam about. During a typical 15 or 30 second commercial, numerous sets of eyeballs are coming and going from the screen for a second or two at a time. Your logo needs to be there when their eyeballs are there.

  A recent Budweiser commercial is a good example. It starts with a close-up shot of the can, which, of course, shows the logo (showing your logo attached to your product is even better than showing it unattached to your product). Throughout the 30-second commercial, the Budweiser logo appears no fewer than six times, including once in huge letters as a crawl (when the word moves across the screen from right to left).

McDonald's does the same thing. You'll often see scenes of people eating in a McDonald's restaurant in which the people are sitting in front of a window with a huge "M" on it. And you see McDonald's bags and drink cups with the logo. McDonald's will often show an outside shot of the store, featuring the huge McDonald's sign front and center.

Most television networks and cable channels superimpose their logos on the screen, usually in the lower right corner, and leave it there during the programming. With viewers surfing through a myriad of channels, how else are people supposed to know what they're watching at any given second? The channel's or network's logo is there whenever their eyes are there.

Also, most television viewers simply don't remember what channel they saw something on. They'll remember what they saw — a story about beached whales that were rescued or whatever — but not remember what channel or program they we're watching at the time. By keeping their logos on the screen as much as possible, television channels make valuable subconscious impressions, which creates top-of-mind awareness, which in turn affects behavior. The same benefits accrue to you in direct proportion to the amount of time your logo appears on the screen.

What if it would appear awkward for your logo to pop up periodically throughout your commercial? Good! One of the ways to make your logo impress inattentive viewers is to let it appear on the screen in various ways, even without any apparent physical or logical attachment to anything else going on. Don't feel your logo needs any logical justification to be shown. Just have it fly by, crawl by, hang there, or be sitting in the corner, even if that seems illogical or awkward. In time, it's awkwardness will dissipate.

- **Step 3: Deliver your point line after one of your logo appearances.** Your point line needn't appear visually. Stating it in the audio track is fine. Just make sure it follows one of your logo appearances any where in your commercial. (The logo may be visual, the point line auditory.)

Your point line will affect many inattentive viewers who

otherwise would have gotten zero message from your commercial. Remember, people — even those in the attentive state — are not scrutinizing or deciphering your commercial to find the message.

- **Step 4: Repeat your company or brand name many times in the audio track.** Television gives you the opportunity to make an impact on the brain from two directions at once, through the eyes and through the ears. Take advantage of the medium's double-barreled impact by delivering your brand name in the audio track, either spoken or sung (jingles are a great simulconsciousing tool).

In many instances, the inattentive viewer will take his eyes off the television screen completely during your commercial. He may even leave the room. But his subconscious mind is still susceptible to impact through sound.

During a recent football telecast I left the room to fetch something from the kitchen when a commercial came on (after I had viewed the first 1.5 seconds or so, by the way). During the time I was in the kitchen, I made a point of consciously listening to the television so as to make it back in time when the game returned. I was in the attentive state as far as the audio portion of the commercial was concerned. But what did I hear? Music. During one 30-second commercial, nothing but music. No announcer, no singing, no words at all providing me with a brand name or point line. Some marketer paid lots of good money to reach people with this commercial, then failed to deliver any message. Evidently he expected people to be sitting in front of the TV set and actually *watching* his commercial. What a disillusioned marketer.

Treating the audio strictly as support for the video is a big mistake. Treating the audio as if it were a radio commercial with no video at all is smart.

HOW TO SIMULCONSCIOUS YOUR RADIO COMMERCIALS

There is no other medium in which simulconsciousing is more important than radio. That's because radio listeners quite often use radio as background sound, with no intent of paying much conscious attention to it. Unlike watching television, when a person consciously shifts back and forth between the attentive and inattentive states, a radio listener may remain in the inattentive state for much longer periods of time.

Once you get the hang of the Simulconscious Strategy, and you've got it working for you in one medium, you will know how to do it in just about every other medium. Here's how it works in radio.

Make sure your radio commercials contain the three simulconscious ad elements: your pre-processed word, brand or company name, and point line. As in television, your pre-processed word and name should be presented in the first 1.5 seconds.

You accomplish most of your simulconsciousing by repeating your name throughout your commercial. Remember, your brand or company may simply pop up embedded in sentences or between sentences without must "justification" for its presence. In one 30-second commercial, your name should be repeated at least six times. Your point line should be presented twice, or four times in a 60-second commercial.

You will be making an impact on the inattentive listener's mind, but don't expect anything except your simulconscious ad elements to get through to them. All that other wonderful, creative verbiage that one can understand only when paying attention will not make an impact on the inattentive listener.

HOW TO SIMULCONSCIOUS IN PRINT

Print includes newspaper and magazine ads, along with direct mail pieces and flyers. As long as you're at it, you may even want to simulconscious in your sales brochures.

I'm sure it comes as no surprise to you that not every person who sees a print ad reads every word of the copy. Very few people do. Therefore, your objective is to provide certain visual elements that catch the eye and make a subconscious impression, even if the person is consciously thinking of something else at the time.

Here's where so many ad designers go wrong. The "eye catching" material they come up with ends up being a large photo or "clever" double-entendre, pay-on-words headline of some kind. Then, after having presumably grabbed the reader's attention, they lead the reader through a thicket of directionless copy, eventually getting around to making the point. Then they plop the logo at the very end, usually in the lower right corner.

Why try so hard to get the reader's attention, require her to spend her valuable time working her way through your copy, and only at the end get around to making the point you want her to get? Do you really expect her to spend the time reading all your copy? And then expend the brainpower necessary to decipher what it is you're trying to get across? Wouldn't it be better, and considerably more effective, to make your point at the very beginning, in a clear, concise fashion, thereby making an impression even when the reader is flipping by and not paying much attention?*

Obviously I can't recommend in this book how your ads, direct mail pieces, or brochures should be designed. But I can give you a design strategy which will at least double the effectiveness of your print ads:

Emphasize the three simulconscious ad elements. Big and bold. You can have additional copy, of course. But consider anything beyond the simulconscious ad elements bonus material that few readers will actually read and comprehend.

Once again, you have constructed your ads to affect people in both the inattentive state (the vast majority) or the attentive state (a lot less).

HOW TO SIMULCONSCIOUS IN BILLBOARDS

You know enough about simulconsciousing now to tell me how to do it. Go ahead, tell me what a simulconscious billboard should look like.

In many cases, all you need on a billboard are two of your simulconscious ad elements, your pre-processed word and logo. Sometimes, you may be able to get your point line in there, too. But don't try to get too much on a billboard. No matter how big they really are, billboards appear rather small when you're driving by. They can appear cluttered very quickly if you're not disciplined enough to leave things out.

Incidently, billboards (and even bumper stickers) are great for making subconscious visual impressions. That's because the subconscious mind is wide open when people are driving. In fact, it's usually the subconscious mind that is doing the driving. Consciously, the driver's mind is on something else entirely, but he or she somehow ends up at home or at work without ever consciously thinking about accelerating, braking, turning, or stopping.

UNINTENTIONAL SIMULCONSCIOUSING

Warning: You may be simulconsciousing your ads or commercials without even knowing you're doing it! That can be very detrimental. You can inadvertently cause negative impressions about your product or service to cement in people's minds, or even help a competitor.

In a Toshiba Copiers television commercial, we see a frustrated, angry office manager trying to get his copying machine to work. He gets so mad at it he dynamites it through the roof. The problem copier is on the screen for almost the entire 30 seconds. Then the Toshiba logo appears and the commercial is over. To the attentive viewer, the point Toshiba is trying to make may be clear: When you have a Toshiba copier, you won't suffer like this poor guy. But in the inattentive viewer's mind, two things are linked: The angry, frustrated guy and Toshiba. See the problem?

This particular advertising format, depicting a problem then offering your product or service as the solution, is very common in advertising. It's also very dangerous. People in the inattentive state can get a completely different message than the one you intend. The only two elements that may make an impression are the problem and your brand name. The problem and your name, linked together.

In the minds of a whole lot of people, *your brand name is the problem!* This is not good.

You must also be extremely cautious if you engage in comparative advertising. If you refer to a competitor by name, or show their logo, you're flirting with real danger is an inattentive environment. While the attentive receiver may grasp your intended message, the inattentive receiver many only notice logos — your competitor's as well as yours.

When Pizza Hut rolled out its delivery service in a major way, it ran a television commercial showing people replacing their Domino's phone number with a Pizza Hut number. Another version showed two Domino's delivery people eating a Pizza Hut pizza for lunch. In these commercials, the Domino's logo appeared as many times as the Pizza Hut logo. To the inattentive viewer, the Domino's logo made just as valid and positive impression as the Pizza Hut logo. Inattentive viewers probably couldn't tell you whether it was a Pizza Hut or Domino's commercial. They simply weren't paying enough attention to get anything but the two brand names.

Speaking of pizza, Papa John's slams Pizza Hut in some of their television commercials, showing the Pizza Hut logo throughout. The U.S. Postal Service shows both FedEx and UPS delivery people, including their respective trucks. An entire Visa commercial features American Express . . . in a negative way, of course. But I guarantee you the inattentive viewer is left with a positive impression of the competitor as much or even more so than of the advertiser.

LET YOUR CREATIVITY FLOURISH WITHIN THE BOUNDS OF THE SIMULCONSCIOUS STRATEGY

The Simulconscious Strategy is not meant to limit creativity. If anything, it requires more creativity to construct an ad or commercial which affects two levels of consciousness instead of just one.

Simulconsciousing is a form of creative discipline. It not only has the advantage of doubling the effectiveness of your advertising at no additional cost, but it keeps your advertising from becoming creatively impotent. Simulconsciousing forces your ad or commercial to be effective, regardless of all the other variables which go into the composition of each and every ad and commercial you craft.

The Simulconscious Strategy is a new and powerful tool for you to use and enjoy. Have fun with it. Let it raise your advertising to a new level of creativity and effectiveness. Let it help your demand flourish!

PART 5

SUSTAINING DEMAND

I'll bet you've heard it said, "Getting to the top is easy, but staying there is the difficult part." While such an expression may keep the troops motivated after a victory, it certainly has no basis in reality. "Getting there" is definitely the difficult part. It's an upward struggle, requiring a great deal of dedication, energy, fortitude, and perseverance, as well as the ability to take hits and recover from setbacks along the way. (Aren't you glad I didn't bring this up at the beginning of the book? You're in too deep to turn back now, pal.)

Standing on the mountain plateau is much easier than the climb it took to get there. Sustaining demand is much easier than creating it. That doesn't mean you can go on automatic pilot and take a nap. Remember prerequisite number one: You must adopt a marketing mindset. That is, you must continue to recognize the importance of marketing and continue to market wisely to sustain success. But unless you manage some major screw-ups (and you and I both know a number of people and companies that seem to display an amazing propensity to do so), you'll sustain demand just fine.

The first chapter in this section is intended to help you keep demand strong and resilient. The second chapter will help prevent you from pulling the royal screw-up.

Chapter Twenty

Maintaining Demand through Reinforcement

Good thing you're sitting down right now. I've got some news that could shake you a bit. *Everyone who buys your product or service harbors some lingering doubt that buying from you is the right thing to do.* Even if they appear to be happy, they have doubt. They may not show it openly, or even admit it to themselves. But somewhere in the back of their minds, they're questioning their decision to buy your product or service.

Hopefully, the doubt is latent or benign. However, doubt has the potential to flare up at any time and become acute. It then affect's the person's thinking and behavior.

Have you ever had a customer or client who went from very satisfied to very unsatisfied overnight? How could they be so happy one minute and so unhappy the next? What happened is this: Their doubt was latent; invisible and innocuous. Then something happened that they didn't like. Perhaps your product didn't work as well as they expected, or your delivery was later than expected, or its color was a slightly different shade than what they had in mind. It could be anything, even something seemingly small or insignificant. But whatever it was they didn't like was enough to cause their doubt to grow. It was enough to tip the scales, where the once benign doubt suddenly became acute and now dominated their thinking.

Doubt in your customers' minds will always be there to some degree. No use trying to eradicate it. However, your objective is to keep the doubt latent; keep it from flaring up and causing harm. Since repeat business from happy customers or clients is critical in demand creation, you must take deliberate measures to squelch doubt and keep it at the innocuous level. This doubt-squelching process is called *reinforcement.*

When you reinforce the purchase decision, you're immunizing the buyer against the growth of doubt. At the same time, you're creating the right mental condition for repeat business, which in turn allows you to encourage endorsement successfully. When you make reinforcement a regular part of your marketing effort, you'll keep demand pumping harder and longer.

WHY DOUBT EXISTS AND GROWS

How does all that doubt get into their minds to begin with? And what causes it to grow? There are three reasons why doubt exists. These are also the three causes that turn benign doubt into malignant doubt.

- •1: **Competitive propaganda.** Your competitor's marketing or sales messages will reach your customers. Some of these messages may be very convincing. The more a competitor's bug swirls around in a person's mind, the more the person questions his decision to buy from you.
- 2: **Blurred judgment.** Many people are simply unable to judge the benefits or results of a product or service accurately. If your company refinishes the hardwood floors in my house, how do I know if you've done a really good job? The floors may look shiny, but how do I know whether they're not supposed to look twice as shiny? How do I know you didn't use some cheap

solution that will ruin the wood within a month? How do I know some other company wouldn't have recommended a different method of restoring the wood, or wouldn't have done the job at a lower price?

The people who buy your product or service may lack the experience and expertise necessary to judge things accurately. This condition, called blurred judgment, is fertile ground for the growth of malignant doubt.

- **3: Unmatched expectation.** For any number of possible reasons, a person may have been under the impression that your product or service would perform differently from what it actually does. The "validity" of their expectation and of their assessment of the result doesn't matter. What does matter is that they were expecting one thing and something else happened. With that unmatched expectation comes increased doubt.

HOW REINFORCEMENT WORKS

After someone buys your product or service, they want to feel they made the right decision. So their brain looks for information that validates or reinforces their buy decision (this happen subconsciously most of the time). It's up to you to supply that reinforcing information! If you don't, you're leaving it up to chance. Remember, they're going to get conflicting information — doubt-provoking information — from your competitors, and you can't let that go unchecked.

When you reinforce the purchase decision, you are supplying information that essentially tells the buyer he or she has done the right thing by buying your item. When you reinforce, you squelch the doubt and keep it at the innocuous level.

TWO TYPES OF REINFORCEMENT

Reinforcement can be of two varieties, internal and external.

Internal reinforcement comes from the actual performance or experience of the product, service, or company itself. For example, you bought a new lawn mower and the salesperson was friendly and helpful, and the mower runs well. Or the restaurant you've chosen provides good service and a great-tasting club sandwich.

External reinforcement comes from any source other than the product or service itself. Perhaps your new lawn mower received an excellent rating in a *Consumer Reports* article. Or a friend you're having lunch with remarks how great the food is at that particular restaurant. External reinforcement can even come from the marketer of the product or service in question. Any reinforcement except that which the actual product's or service's performance provides is external.

I've got a question for you. Which type of reinforcement, internal or external, is stronger? Which has the bigger effect on people? For most people most of the time, external reinforcement is much stronger. There have been umpteen psychological studies done over many years that shows how people's opinions can be shaped, even changed, by what other people think.

People are very susceptible to external opinion right after they decide to purchase from you. Another reason why you need to provide that reinforcement.

HOW TO REINFORCE THE PURCHASE DECISION

Reinforcement can come from three different angles: supreme execution and follow-through, printed materials, and in your advertising. (A fourth is good old word-of-mouth. Hopefully that is happening, but it's out of your direct control. The three presented here are under your direct control.)

Here are some step-by-step procedures for tapping into all three:
- **Step 1: Give the buyer more than they expect.** If your package says it contains 16 ounces, make sure it actually contains 16.5 or 17 ounces. If your package of baseball cards says there are 14 in the pack, put 15 in some of the packages. If you agreed to finish a job on the 18th of the month, finish it on the 15th. If they're buying one day's worth of your consulting, give them some extra follow-up attention at no additional cost.

  The idea is to nip doubt in the bud by making a positive and *unexpected* impression at the time the buyer takes possession of your product or service. The key to making this work is that it must be unexpected. The buyer must be surprised that she got more than she paid for.

I'm not saying you shouldn't package creatively and hype the deal. That's good from a marketing standpoint, but it's not reinforcement. By definition, reinforcement can only occur after someone purchases. You need to hold some advantage or benefit back so you can surprise the buyer with it after they buy.

- **Step 2: Create printed reinforcement materials.** Remember when your company refinished my hardwood floors and I harbored some doubt about your work? Do you think my doubt would have diminished if, after I had signed the work order, you provided me with a brochure explaining how the process works, how to judge results, and how to best maintain the floor? And would my doubt have diminished even further if, upon completing the work, you handed me a printed guarantee?

With written materials, you can address each of the doubt-breeding conditions: competitive propaganda, blurred judgment, and unmatched expectations. Educate people on the proper way to judge results. Tell them exactly what to expect. And reassure them they got the best quality and/or deal on the market.

Isn't it odd how each of us receives a good amount of literature before the purchase, but next to none afterward? If you've got lots of printed sales material, that's fine. But it's just that: sales material. It is not reinforcement material. And you need printed reinforcement materials.

Here are some examples:

I bought a suit at the Men's Warehouse recently. A week or so later a Thank You card arrived in the mail, along with a note from the salesperson and his business card attached. (Thank You notes are always good, but they're just the first step. Once you've got a buyer's name and address in your database, work 'em!)

After I purchased a camcorder at Circuit City, they slipped my sales receipt inside a small folder. The folder contained information on Circuit City's "No Lemon Guarantee," their factory-authorized service centers, their return policy, and a special toll-free number to call if I needed help setting up or using the item. Wow! Does that make me feel I bought from the right place? Absolutely.

I bought a rather pricey, replacement door knocker for my front door a couple years ago. In the package was an eight-page, full-color booklet containing information on the proper care of fine brass, the historical significance of Baldwin Hardware (the manufacturer), Baldwin's "commitment to you" (the guarantee), and where to get additional help if I need it. Remember, this is a simple door knocker. One moving part, and all you do is lift it and slam it back down. But the reinforcement material is about as psychologically high-tech as you can get.

- **Step 3: Reinforce in your advertising.** Yes, advertising's primary objective is to stimulate demand, to increase sales. But it can also reinforce. Much like we learned with the Simulconscious Strategy, where the receiver of the message determines at which consciousness level the message will be received, the receiver can also determine whether an ad or commercial sells them or reinforces them. Simply put, if they haven't bought your product or service yet, your advertising may very well influence them to do so. If they have already purchased, your advertising may reinforce that purchase. (By the way, people will pay closer attention to an ad or commercial *after* they purchased the item being advertised, so using your ads to reinforce is a natural.)

  AT&T's slogan, "AT&T. The Right Choice," is an excellent use of reinforcement in advertising. The tag line alone does the trick. It blatantly tells people that when they choose AT&T, they've made the right choice. Key point: People won't remember where they got the idea, they won't remember who told them AT&T was the right choice. They just know that choosing AT&T makes them feel confident, secure; that they've made the right purchase decision.

Chapter Twenty-one

Preventing Demand Disintegration

Demand doesn't increase forever. Eventually it will level off somewhat; things will slow down. It's one of the natural laws of the universe, and there's nothing you can do to alter that.

However, there are things you can do to cause demand to level off much sooner than it otherwise might. In fact, there are things you can do that cause demand to screech to a halt. All of these things fall under the heading of screwing up. Believe me, no matter how high your demand jet is flying at the moment, it can crash and burn in no time if you screw up big enough.

Of all the pitfalls out there, there are only five that are lethal enough to destroy you (excluding doing something illegal or immoral). To guard against their clutches, you must recognize them, then defend yourself against them. Otherwise, there's a good chance you'll fall victim sooner or later.

PITFALL NUMBER ONE: THE DOWNWARD SPIRAL

As I stated, demand doesn't grow like crazy forever. A number of factors can cause demand for your product or service to sputter at times. A new competitor pops up, the economy tightens, a piece of bad publicity bites, or your product simply reaches maturity. The critical factor is not why or even when demand will slow down, but *how you react to the slowdown* when it arrives.

An all-too-common pitfall that destroys many marketers is the *downward spiral trap*. Here's the lethal scenario. As demand slows and revenues decline, profit margins become squeezed. Once you've become accustomed to a particular profit margin and planned your budgets accordingly, it's extremely difficult to accept any less. So the marketer adjusts the logical way — he cuts expenses to maintain margins. The area that seems most susceptible to budget cuts is marketing (it's a heck of a lot easier picking up the phone and can-celling some ad schedule than it is firing people or taking away perks). In accounting parlance, advertising and promotion fall into the "discretionary expense" category, meaning they can be reduced or cut without adversely affecting operations.

The accountants are partly right. Under certain conditions, you can reduce your marketing expenses and suffer few harmful conse-quences in the short run. It's called *coasting*. The pilot can cut back on the throttle, yet the jet still streaks through the sky, its momen-tum propelling it along as though no cutback occurred.

With momentum, your revenues can be maintained for a while even though you cut back on your marketing throttle. In other words, because of momentum, there's a *time lag* between the reduction in your marketing activity and the decline of your revenues. This time lag can create the false impression that a healthy amount of market-ing is not necessary. However, it doesn't take long before your mo-mentum slows and the time lag runs out. Revenues now indeed begin to fall.

As revenues decrease further in our scenario, the marketer ad-justs by cutting expenses further. Since the time lag that once ex-isted between reduced marketing activity and falling demand has long since evaporated, an immediate decline in revenue results. The marketer reacts by cutting expenses further. The process repeats until revenue, and demand, have fallen below the point of no return.

Once you're caught in the downward spiral, it's almost impossible to get out. A tremendous amount of marketing power is required to reverse your downward fall and climb back. The odds of pulling your demand jet out of its tailspin are overwhelmingly against you. (In fact, you may not be around to attempt it. They may replace you with someone that is mandated to "turn it around.")

The best way to survive the downward spiral is to avoid getting caught in it in the first place. If you must coast, do so for only a brief period. Better yet, maintain marketing expenditures even in tough times. It's not always easy, but it is much safer.

PITFALL NUMBER TWO: COMPETITOR FIXATION

Have you noticed that throughout this book, I've spoken very little about the competition? The reason is this: Too many marketers spend too much time worrying too much about what their competitors are doing instead of concentrating on what they themselves are doing, or should be doing.

Paying an inordinate amount of attention to a competitor is called *competitor fixation*. It's a condition you want to avoid.*

Does this mean you should ignore your competitors? Sometimes yes. Sometimes no. While it makes perfect sense to maintain an awareness of what your competitors are up to, be careful. You can find yourself so focused on a competitor you lose sight of everything else.

Your competitors are going to do what's best for them, and you've got to do what's best for you. You've got to keep your eye on the ball — your consumers or customers — and not have your attention diverted by a dazzling or taunting competitor, especially a weak one.

Victims of competitor fixation lose their ability to think rationally. Rather than looking after themselves, they end up making decisions designed primarily to thwart a competitor (the two are rarely one

---

*Even my speech entitled "Competitive Intuition" has little to do with the competition and a lot to do with you and your customers.

and the same). They become so caught up in this "killer mentality," they live for beating the competition in every possible way. Many victims of competitor fixation even allow their thwarting efforts to slip below ethical boundaries, unfortunately.

You don't have to expend undue energy trying to inflict pain on your competitors. They will either prosper or suffer on their own without your intervention. Take Sam Walton as an example. The late founder of Wal-Mart would occasionally walk into a competing store and check it out. He'd take some notes, evaluate what he saw, even get an idea or two. But that's about it. In 1990, when Wal-Mart surpassed Sears and became the number one retailer in the United States, *USA Today* asked Sam for a comment on the triumph. "We're not in the business to beat Sears," he stated. Beating Sears was never a goal at Wal-Mart. Serving its customers the best it could was the goal.

The real idea is to suck your competitors into fixating on you, not you on them. Once they begin stalking you and reacting to your every move, you know you've got 'em . Just continue to do what's best for you and your customers, and let the competitive situation take care of itself.

PITFALL NUMBER THREE: INTERNAL STRIFE

Like pitfall number one, this pitfall is an inappropriate reaction to a natural slowdown or glitch in demand and revenues.

When revenues slow down, people within an organization often panic. They start changing the very things that made them successful. They start doubting themselves. They begin arguing among themselves, often creating internal turmoil that renders their future marketing moves tentative and weak. They fall victim to the pitfall of *internal strife*.

Internal strife is a cancer that weakens you tremendously. It's caused by people within an organization who continually doubt or cast aspersions upon their own marketing efforts. Even one doubter can cause constant conflict, ultimately weakening the organization to the point of inhibiting success.

There is a time and place for dissent and disagreement. That time is before you put a particular plan into effect, before the action starts. Like the way the United States government functions before taking military action. The president, along with other members of the executive branch, confer with Congress, solicit opinion from foreign leaders, and ascertain the sentiment of the American people. Then they make decisions and act. Disagreement may still exist, but most Americans will support the military anyway so as to make it effective.

Once the action starts, and you've got people, money, and other resources on the line, it's time to stop arguing and become a cooperating team dedicated to accomplishing the objective.

Marketing is very subjective and inherently rhetorical. Everyone has a different opinion, and debate is never ending. In addition, not every move you make will be successful; setbacks will occur. In the midst of all that, it really boils down to this: Will your people remain committed, focused, harmonious, and strong . . . or will you constantly question, doubt, argue, or buckle?

PITFALL NUMBER FOUR: FAILURE TO REINVEST

At last, demand for your kloptigobinators is at stratospheric height and the money's rolling in. Now you're in the position to do what you've always dreamed of. In rapid succession you move the company into the stateliest of quarters, purchase a corporate jet, acquire an unrelated business, and hire a slew of middle managers with their own administrative assistants. Likewise, you make magnificent additions to your personal antique car, yacht, and Asian art collections. In short, you do everything with the profits except reinvest in the product or service that produced the profit.

People are entitled do the spoils, no doubt. But a person shouldn't starve the golden goose to death in the process. Any successful product, service, or business will remain successful only through constant reinvestment.

I'll bet you can name at least one small business owner or large corporate CEO who siphons off all the profits for who-knows-what. They may be glowing in some short-term, fifteen-minute spotlight now, but it will catch up with them sooner or later when the cash cow is wrung dry and no longer produces.

Your products and/or services require some of the cash they produced returned back to them to continue growing — or to just maintain the existing sales level. This means increased expenditures for product/service improvement and marketing, not less. Avoiding the *failure to reinvest* pitfall is simply a matter of keeping the golden goose properly fed.

PITFALL NUMBER FIVE: HUBRIS

Ask anyone who has had his or her once high-flying success crumble to nothing what the lesson of the experience has been, and chances are the answer will be "humility."

You don't have to learn the hard way. While your business is still thriving, take a moment to recognize a few realities. Recognize that some of your success is due to sheer luck. Recognize that success in one area or endeavor is not always transferable into another, different area. Recognize that things totally out of your control can come along and have a major adverse effect on you at any time. Recognize that your wisdom in knowing when to hold 'em and when to fold 'em plays a major role in the scheme of things.

Laws change, people die, technology advances, products and services fall in and out of style, the economy tightens, catastrophes occur. Anything can happen.

Be grateful for what you have. Share your success with others. Show appreciation to others, and reward the people who consistently contribute to your success. In short, carry a tad of humility rather than hubris with you. When you do, your chances of maintaining success over the long run are much greater.

PART 6

GETTING HELP

Who will do all your marketing strategizing, planning, creating, and executing? Besides you and/or any number of people in your organization, you'll most likely require some form of outside help. Marketing is just too important to go it alone.

The most common source of help is the advertising agency. If you have an agency, or are thinking of hiring one, the first chapter in this part is designed to help you get the most from your agency.

Help is also available from any number of other sources, including consultants, freelancers, media outlets themselves, and production houses that specialize in a specific media such as television commercials or direct mail campaigns. The second chapter will bring these sources into focus.

The final chapter is designed to help you help yourself succeed. You'll learn about two key ingredients that are necessary to make all you've read about thus far really effective.

Chapter Twenty-two

The Truth about Ad Agencies

The truth is, there are some very good people doing some very good work at some very good ad agencies. The truth is, a good agency will probably help you more than it'll hurt you.

So why is there such an abundance of mediocre, even downright terrible, advertising out there? With predominantly good quality going in, you'd expect better quality coming out, wouldn't you? Something is amiss. Let's determine exactly where the problem lies so you can guard against its consequences.

FLAWS IN THE AGENCY SYSTEM

All fingers point to the system under which advertising agencies, and their clients, operate. Specifically, there are three fundamental flaws in the system.

Flaw Number One: Account Pitching.

Agencies end up spending a big chunk of time, energy, and money creating pro forma campaigns for accounts they hope to "win." (An "account," from an agency's perspective, is a product or service with an advertising budget.) That is, they must arrive at your door with a well-defined strategy and campaign — two items of vital importance — already created just to make an appeal for your business.

Wouldn't all that time, energy, and money an agency spends on account pitching be better spent serving its existing accounts instead? Would you rather have your agency spending their time, energy, and money on your account or on pitching some new account? The agencies are the first to admit this pitching process is a lousy way to go, but they're forced into it. Why?

Because clients love to be pitched. They've long discovered that the utterance of three magic words, "up for review," instantly produces a hoard of salivating agencies panting at the door. The client (or potential client, as the case may be) extends "offers to pitch" to a number of interested agencies, then sits back and watches the fun.

The agencies all dive into grindstone mode and come up with their individual strategies and campaigns, which can take weeks or months. Each agency, pressure-pitted against one another, eventually puts on an elaborate, expensive song and dance to a group of reveling executives comfortably perched on their thrones of power, hooting and howling between swigs of spirited libation.*

I'm convinced companies promulgate this system and force agencies into creative shootouts for two main reasons. First, because they themselves have to suck-up to their own clients or customers day in and day out, it feels good to make someone suck-up to them once in a while. They seem to enjoy the role reversal very, very, very much.

Second, they see other companies demanding to be pitched, so they figure that must be the way it's done. "If the agency put on an

---

*Yes, this really happens. Then again, sometimes the opposite happens. Sometimes the client maintains a stone-cold poker face and gives the agency no indication of pleasure, which may be even worse.

exotic dog-and-pony show for those other guys, they should do the same for me," the thinking goes.

Yet under this account pitching system, hiring an ad agency has degenerated into a major sucking-up contest. Do you really believe this pitching process results in a higher caliber of work that will benefit you, the client? If so, then you may as well hire your medical doctor, legal council, and accounting firm the same way. "But it's not done that way in those industries," you point out. Ah, perhaps there is a good reason.

Flaw Number Two: Award-Winning Mentality.

Human nature dictates that we all want recognition, respect, and admiration for the work we do. The ego-intensive advertising business is no exception. (A healthy ego is not necessarily a problem, as long as one keeps one's ego on a short leash. Often the people with the biggest egos turn out the best work.)

Embedded in the minds of ad agency personnel is an ever-present, unquenchable desire to create advertising that wins awards. Ever see a 30-second television commercial followed by a 30-second roll of credits? Neither have I. In advertising, the recognition comes from winning awards, not from exposure in the ads themselves.

This would be fine if the award-winning advertising were the same as the sales-generating advertising. The truth is, however, that what wins awards often does not sell product, and vice-versa. In fact, the ads and commercials that win the major awards are often the biggest failures in terms of affecting sales of the products or services they're supposed to be promoting.

In the late '90s, Nissan ran a campaign that won numerous awards from the ad community. The television commercials showed G.I.-Joe and Barbie-style dolls driving off in a sports car as Van Halen's "You Really Got Me" bellowed forth. Another one had a dog driving his master's reclining chair through the streets and to the Nissan showroom. Clever, creative stuff. Only it didn't sell cars or trucks. The dealers complained, and the campaign was scrapped.

Many marketers are surprised — sometimes shocked — to find out that the criteria for determining award-worthy advertising have nothing to do with the sales results of the product or service being advertised.* Rather, the criteria involves the composition or makeup of the ads or commercials — theme, copywriting, artwork, direction, etc.

In some cases, an ad or commercial can be considered absolute crap, a creative abomination, by the ad community. Yet it can be extremely effective. Wisk's age-old "Ring Around The Collar" campaign is a classic example. An artistic dud by any award-determining criterion, but it sells loads of Wisk.

Agencies create advertising to win awards because that's there the recognition comes from. Of course they care about product sales, too. After all, the whole purpose of advertising is to stimulate demand and sales of the product or service in question. But make no mistake about it, increased sales of a product can still leave the agency dry of recognition and admiration. How so? Look what happens when a product or service becomes a big seller. The company or marketer (the agency's client) takes all the credit. Mushrooming sales must be due to the superiority of the product or service, or to the client's intelligence and managerial talent, right? As for the ad agency, their reward is to keep the account for a while longer. No wonder they look beyond sales results for recognition.

Flaw Number Three: The Client-As-Expert Mentality

It's not commonly expressed outside the advertising fraternity, but if you could ask an agency off the record what its biggest obstacle usually is, chances are it would tell you it's their clients themselves. And that's if you talk to account executives, who are generally very diplomatic people. Talk to creative people and you'll hear roaring horror stories about how their entire work has been so mangled and mutilated by clients that they couldn't even recognize it in the end.

(In the section above, I implied the agency may require client supervision so it doesn't create advertising designed to win awards at the expense of advertising designed to sell product. In this sec-

*The American Marketing Association's Effie award is a notable exception. It is awarded based solely on the effectiveness and results of a marketing campaign. If there is an award that really counts, this is the one.

tion, we're looking at the other side of the coin, the meddling client that turns the agency's good work into mediocre muck.)

Who's right and who's wrong — the agency or the client? Each party is likely right about half the time (and what constitutes "right" is very subjective, keep in mind). Probably you know more about your business than any agency will ever know, and your agency knows more about advertising than you'll ever know. This makes a strong argument for a client-agency relationship built on mutual respect and decisions by consensus.

But a funny thing happens to people when they start dealing with advertising. The same person who believes he needs outside expertise in the areas of medicine, law, or accounting for some reason believes he possesses all the expertise necessary when it comes to advertising. Since marketers of this mindset believe they know how to create advertising, they tend to view their agency not as collaborators, but as mere executors. Their personal objective is to see that the agency simply carries out their orders. As you might expect, the result most often is an ineffectual piece of advertising mediocrity.

HOW TO GET THE MOST OUT OF YOUR AGENCY

You suffer from the flawed system only if you abide by the flawed system. There are no rules or laws forcing you to do so in advertising. You, the client, have the power to operate differently, and you don't have to spearhead a movement to revolutionize the entire advertising industry to do so. Simply do what's best for you, and forget about how everyone else chooses to operate. And remind yourself that you are not alone in choosing to do things differently. Since the original edition of this book first appeared in 1991, more and more marketers are doing what we're about to discuss.

Choosing an Ad Agency

- **Step 1: Narrow down your choice of agencies to two or three before contacting them.** Find ads and commercials you really like, and find out what agencies produced them. If they've demonstrated ability and skill under varying circumstances for other clients, chances are they can do the same for you.

Don't rule out new agencies, either. Although they may not have a track record of success to show, they may make up for it in enthusiasm, desire, and talent. Your account may be more important to them than it would be to a larger, established agency (this is especially true if you are a rather small account, meaning your ad budget is not large enough to excite the bigger agencies). You can locate new agencies simply by calling your local ad club.

- **Step 2: Talk to your two or three choices.** Your objective is to (a) find an agency that will gain an overall understanding of your situation, and (b) be a good match or fit with you. To do this, tell them about your business and what you're trying to accomplish. See how well they listen. Ask about their philosophies and working methods. Don't put them in a position of having to offer advice this early in the game. You haven't engaged their services yet, so don't expect them to come up with any answers yet.

  And don't get caught up in agency pitches! Pitting one agency against another in speculative matches is a big waste of everyone's time and money. Your chances of hiring the best agency for you decrease with pitches. Your chances of hiring the best agency for you increase with one-on-one rapport and understanding.

Working With Your Agency

Here are some tips, in no particular order.

- **Discuss your targeted Influence Types early on.** The agency should have a good understanding of Influence Types, The Influence Graph, and how your product, service, or company meshes with certain Influence Types at this point in time (Chapters 15 and 16).

  Discussing this early on will prevent the agency from creating ads and commercials that mismatch your targeted Influence Types. Let's say you expect a fairly traditional, conservative-looking ad that will appeal to right-sided Type Threes and Type Fours, and your agency unveils a stylish, super-trendy ad with decidedly Type One and Two appeal. Oops. Best to discuss all this going in, rather than the two of you ending up deeply down different paths.

- **Offer recognition.** Share your success with your agency. The idea is for you to provide some recognition so the agency doesn't feel so compelled to get the recognition elsewhere (like award winning). The way(s) you choose to demonstrate your appreciation can be many and varied. Here are some possibilities:

  Mention its name when you're interviewed by the press about your success.

  Why not create your own award and present it to your agency? That's a major credibility booster any agency would cherish. (At the same time, let them know you will not be impressed if their work wins any award not based on effectiveness.)

  Allow your agency to cite before-and-after sales results as evidence of their fine work.

  Do you pay your agency a bonus based on predetermined levels of sales achieved?

  Do you invite your agency people to any of your staff parties?

  Ninety-nine percent of all clients fail to offer their agency any recognition or reward beyond simply paying their bills, and all too many are slow to do even that. Herein lies a major opportunity for you. If you do the opposite, and offer recognition and reward, you can quickly become the dream client every agency hopes to find some day. On which account do you think your agency will want to spend most of their time and effort? Yours, or the other 99 percent who don't show any appreciation? Once word gets out you operate this way, how many other agencies will call and express an interest in you? The better you treat your agency, the more motivated they become to please you.

- **Don't change too many things.** Your agency will be showing you ideas, concepts, and designs along the way. At various times throughout the process, you should feel free to express your desires, concerns, and opinions. This is expected, desired.

Just don't overdo it. A design change here, a copy alteration there, fine. But you've got to resist the temptation to order change upon change, redo after redo. If you find yourself asking for hefty makeovers, something is wrong with your approach or managing style.

Perhaps you didn't communicate properly at the outset. Setting parameters and articulating your preferred "look and feel" is essential.

Or perhaps you're afflicted by *Gotta-Change-Something Disease*. Marketers with this disease feel compelled to demand constant changes, regardless of merit. The primary symptoms are comments like these:

"Find another actor."

"Make the picture bigger and the type smaller."

"Make the type bigger and the picture smaller."

"The woman should be wearing a green dress, not a red dress."

"The (fill in the blank) is okay, but the (fill in the blank) has got to go."

People display Gotta-Change-Something Disease because they subconsciously feel a need to affirm their position or flex their authority. It's a power move, simply put.

Secure, self-assured people aren't so afflicted. They know they get the best work out of their agency by displaying trust in the agency's judgment, not by displaying doubt through token changes. (Of course, an error or technical mistake always deserves correction.)

Chapter Twenty-three

Production Houses, Freelancers, Consultants, etc.

The biggest advantage of the advertising agency is that they do it all for you. They create, coordinate, and execute. All you do is supervise and pay the bills.

There are alternatives, however. Alternative methods and sources of everything from copywriting, artwork, media buying, direct mail promotions, contests, strategic planning, audio and video production, etc. For any number of reasons, not the least of which is to save substantial dollars, you may prefer to purchase various marketing services à la carte from a variety of sources. Let's look at some of the best types of sources.

Production Houses

An independent "production house" is a general term for firms that provide a specific marketing product or service (the word "independent" means they are not formally connected with any media outlet or ad agency). For example, you can have your radio or television commercial produced by a company that specializes in exactly that. The particular production company you hire can in turn hire the writer, talent, director, etc. When each job is completed, the production company will hand you the finished product in your preferred form (film, tape, disk, whatever) and you do with it what you like.

Let's say you're producing a brochure with multiple photos of models using products. No matter how great your models and products look, and no matter how good your photographer, the photos will need enhancement. (Like taking out a dimple. Or replacing a model's closed eyes in one shot with her open eyes from another shot. Or replacing the bland studio background with a lavish outdoor background.) Where would you go to have this type of work done? An independent production house such as Grunis Studios in Madison Heights, Michigan. Photo retouching is precisely what they do. (You would be amazed what kind of photo enhancements can be done when you combine artists with computers.)

You can purchase specific direct mail campaigns from companies that specialize in direct mail marketing/advertising. They will customize everything for you, including the copy, artwork, printing, mailing list, and the actual mailing of the pieces. We're talking start-to-finish turn-key production.

Many production houses cater to particular industries. You can often find them listed in trade publications or directories (printed or online), or your company may indeed receive mailings from them from time to time. Your handy yellow pages has local production houses listed under headings like "Audio-Visual Production Services," or "Advertising, Direct Mail," or "Graphic Designers."

Freelancers

Every medium-sized and larger city in the nation has a cadre of freelance production people, including copywriters, designers, artists, photographers, voiceover talent, actors, models, etc. They are hired by the job or project.

You'll find some of them listed under the headings "Writers,"

"Artists," "Photographers," etc. in the yellow pages. Interestingly however, many freelance professionals operate below the radar screen, making them hard to find at times. For instance, the photo of me on the cover of this book was taken by Robert Ziegler, a commercial photographer, and the cover art was done by Brenda Shelton Martin, a graphic artist. Both Robert and Brenda are top-notch professionals, yet neither has more than an obscure, one-line listing somewhere in the phone book. (They get business mainly through reputation and referral.)

Collect and save the names of freelancers whenever you come across them (and you will once you train your brain to be on the lookout). Then you can refer to your "source" list whenever the need arises. You may also want to ask around for recommendations. Or, if the person you call initially does not do what you have in mind, ask them to recommend someone who does.

Service Bureaus

Service Bureaus handle computerized graphics. They can provide you with high resolution scans and printouts, color matchprints or transparencies, color separated negatives, etc. You have to have some graphic knowledge and skill to prepare your materials properly before handing it over to a service bureau. But if you know what you're doing, they'll be indispensable. Look under the yellow pages heading "Desktop Publishing" for service bureaus in your area.

Media Buying Services

Media buying services will "place" your ad or commercial on the optimum media outlets according to your objectives and budget. They know how to negotiate the best deals, how to get the most exposure for your money. They are paid a flat fee by the client (you), or if your placements are large enough, media buying services may forgo the fee entirely and be adequately compensated by their standard 15 percent commission paid by the media outlets they buy.

One word of caution. In some organizations, media buying is considered a low-level task that they relegate to some barely-out-of-their-teens neophyte who is learning by mistake as they spend your money. If you use a media buying service (or the media buying services of an ad agency), make sure the person doing the actual buying is a seasoned veteran, someone who's been in the media trenches.

Media Outlets

A great source for advertising assistance, especially for small businesses that may not be able to afford an array of out-sourced suppliers, is the actual media outlets themselves. Most media outlets have copywriters, artists, and talent on staff for this exact purpose.

Radio stations, television stations, and cable TV systems will produce your commercials for you at nominal cost or even no cost (provided you buy time on their stations, of course).

Many newspapers, magazines, direct mail couponers, and billboard companies will do the same.

Only two possible drawbacks. One, the production is usually low-budget stuff. No television station, for example, is going to produce some razzle-dazzle, state-of-the-art commercial that would otherwise cost you three-quarters of a million dollars on the open market to have done, and hand it to you free of charge (they are most likely not even capable of such work).

Two, media outlets have a limited ability to offer high-level strategic analysis, comprehensive marketing planning, or multimedia campaign design. They operate on a much shallower plain, producing simple ads or commercials that come and go.

Consultants

Where do you find savvy, original thinkers who can develop an integral understanding of your company and provide the high-level strategizing and planning you may desire? Consultants. Management, marketing, or media consultants.

Many consultants are also speakers and authors. Which makes it relatively easy for you to find the consultant best suited to your needs. You can sample a consultant's philosophies and methodologies via their seminars, books, tapes, etc., then contact the one you like.

Chapter Twenty-four

The Key Ingredients That Make it All Work

Human nature is human nature. The human brain works today the same as it has since the beginning of humanity and is unlikely to change. That's why the material in this book works so well. All of the strategies and techniques I've described are based on immutable principles of human psychology, principles that I did not invent or discover. I merely analyzed them and found ways in which they can be used to market effectively. Therefore, except for a few small tidbits, the material in this book is timeless. It will work for you today as well as at any time in the future.

But there are two major ingredients missing from this book. Ingredients so important and necessary that without them, none of the strategies and techniques will work for you. I would gladly have supplied these marvelous ingredients if that were possible, but their nature is such that they cannot be contained in this book. The two key ingredients that makes it all work are your *creativity* and *execution*. And *you* are obviously the only person that can supply them.

When you add your creativity and execution, everything comes alive and demand is indeed created.

As I said in the Preface, one of my objectives was to get you thinking; to stimulate your creativity. That's half of it. The other half is implementing and executing. My guess is that you've been implementing some of the things you learned as you read. And now that you've come to the end of the book, I want to challenge you to take as much of this material as you can and mold it to fit your particular situation. Create new twists and methods. Have fun with it.

In addition, feel good about your progress, both professionally and personally. If you've read this book from cover to cover, you know more about marketing than most. Your knowledge is already showing, not only in the results you're producing, but in your ability to discuss and persuade.

The powerful strategies and techniques contained in this book, combined with your creativity and execution, are omnipotent. And you are now at the forefront of it all. You are indeed creating demand and enjoying its mighty rewards!

Index

Black & Decker, 30
Bloomingdales, 173
Blurred judgment, 220-21
BMW, 57, 193
Boone's Farm wine, 39n
Bowie, David, 28
Boy George, 28
Boy Scouts, 56
Brand preference, 85, 147
Brooks, Garth, 173
Brunswick, Georgia, 77
Brunswick, Virginia, 77
Budweiser, 61, 208
Burger King, 7, 30
Bush, George, 74
Buyer's remorse, 101
Buying habit, 85, 89, 138

C

Calvin Klein clothes, 51
Carlin, George, 185
Casablanca records, 27
Casino Windsor, 116
Categorization, 109
CBS network, 18, 134
Celebrities, 60
Chemlawn, 154
Chevrolet, 7, 151
Chiquita bananas, 154
CHR format, 3, 169
Christian Doir, 173
Christmas, 23, 48, 70
Chrysler, 7
Circuit City, 223
Clark, Dick, 101
Claussen pickles, 31
Client-as-expert mentality, 236-37
Clutter Buster Strategy, 195-96
CNN, 39
Coasting, 226-27
Coca-Cola, 39-40, 49, 51- 52, 112, 114, 187
Collected impressions, 88-89
Columbia House, 150
Comfort button, 160, 162-63
Comfort Inn, 116
Comparative advertising, 187, 214

"Competitive Intuition" speech, 227n
Competitive propaganda, 220
Competitor fixation, 4, 227-28
Computer City, 116
Confusion, 11-12, 36-37
Consultants, 244
Consumer Reports magazine, 222
Container differences, 27-28
Contests, 22-24
  direct mail, 136, 138-39
  large prizes without mass market exposure, 43-44
  multiple payoffs from, 24
  as promotions, 14
  running, 24
  types of, 23
  value of, 22
Convenience, 128
Converse shoes, 121
Cooper, Alice, 28
Coors beer, 76, 179, 180
Coors, Peter, 180
Copy
  and emotion-logic conflict, 104-5
  persuasive, 134, 138
  projection in, 95
  Simulconscious Strategy in, 210-11
Core consumers, 120
Core Obsession Trap, 122-23
  disadvantages of, 122
  as a waste of money, 42-43, 121-24
Core Maximization Level, 124
Co-sponsored promotions, 14, 23
Costas, Bob, 36
Coupons, 136, 137-38
Craftsman tools, 54
Crazed Complicator, 11-12
Creativity, 37, 214-15, 223, 235-36, 238, 241, 245-46
Cross pen, 152
Cross-promotion, 146
Cuisinart, 59
Customer grading questionnaire, 38

D

"Dateline," 19
Deals. *See also* Expensive-Deal